HINDU
Caste, Custom and Ceremony

HINDU
Caste, Custom and Ceremony

PROF. (DR.) CHITRALEKHA SINGH
D.LIT
PREM NATH

PATHAK PUBLISHER AND DISTRIBUTORS
New Delhi (INDIA)

HINDU: Caste, Custom and Ceremony

Author : Prof. (Dr.) Chitralekha Singh, Prem Nath

ISBN : 978-93-48824-79-0

Price : 1195/-

First Edition: 2025

Published by :
PATHAK PUBLISHER AND DISTRIBUTORS
E-6/33c & 34, Ground Floor, Sangam Vihar
New Delhi-110080
E-mail: pathakppd@gmail.com

Typographic Design by: G. R. Sharma

Printed in India

CONTENTS

Preface	vii
1. Introduction	1
2. The Sacraments	11
3. Marriage	23
4. Death and Funeral Rites	73
5. Shraddh - Ancestor Worship	105
6. Hindu Pregnancy and Childbirth Rites	123
7. Name Giving Ceremony	137
8. Building Ceremonies	145
9. The Pilgrimage: Holy Places	155
10. Tribal Customs and Ceremonies	173
Appendix	181
Bibliography	185
Glossary	186

PREFACE

THE SCRIPTURES, the study of sacred books, throw light on the philosophical texts and the performance of *Samskaras*. The *Vedas*, the fountain head of Indian glory, which are divine revelations, codified by Vyasa, give the message through many other works. The scriptures contain the details of man's religious duties, the rites and rituals he should perform, customs, traditions and all other details help him to keep his mind pure and to enable him to do good only and eschew evil. All the sacraments are in Sanskrit and thus Sanskrit plays a main role. Spiritual exercises, singing hymns and visiting temples are necessary, but if devotion is combined with the observance of these duties, the benefits will be far greater and the mind can be cleared of all impurities.

In ancient days, everyone used to conduct worship in his house (as noted by Hanuman in Vibhishan's place in Sri Lanka or in various dramatic scenes in the *Mahabharata, Ramayana, Sri K'rsna* performed in television serials) and carried out other duties and went to temples.

The aim of this book is to apprise the human being to utilize his privileged rare faculty of reasoning and discriminating between good and evil. The study of traditional sacraments described herein, aim at one's utilizing the rare opportunity to rise to the level of the divine.

In the present times, when a man is so busy in his materialistic adventures, all that one can do is to study scriptures, carry out worship in the house and when time permits, visit temples and attend sermons by saints. Devotion at all occasions is essentially desired.

The description of customs and ceremonies, given in this book, is brief and not exhaustive. If one were to describe each in details, it would require many volumes; but the details, howsoever little given in this book, will be found useful by the reader to enlighten his mind.

The authors are grateful to Shri Suman Pathak, Director, Pathak Publisher and Distributors for his constant encouragement and critical review from time to time. Shri Pathak has been so kind to see the timely and beautiful publication of this book through Pathak Publisher and Distributor, New Delhi

Readers are requested to inform the authors about any shortcomings in the book, so that improvement can be done in the next edition.

Chitralekha Singh

CHAPTER I
Introduction

India is basically a country of religion. Here every aspect of life is governed by religion. As Indians have been living on the mercy of nature, the elements of nature have become part of religion in this country. Farmers, who form sixty per cent of Indian population, are basically religious and conservative in outlook. Apart from it, there is a dearth of education in Indian village society and it makes people more religious. As Gillin and Gillin have said, "The social field of religion may be regarded as including those emotionalized beliefs prevalent in a social group concurring the supernatural plus crest and behaviours, material objects and symbols associated with such beliefs." All the writers and sociologists, who have defined religion, have agreed in common faith in the existence of some superior power in the core of every religion.

Almost all aspects of life are influenced by religion, which is an important part of culture and civilization. In India, the forms of religion at the national and local levels are different. At the national level there is Hinduism derived from the philosophical system of India, which is called *dharma*. At the local or village level, the form of religion is different, which includes various elements of small tradition. Thus the national form of religion is based on classical customs and traditions, while the local forms are dominated by the elements from small tradition.

Indian religion contains a worldly outlook and regulations and influence of the world form a part of the religion. As such religion contains views about magic, sorcery, taboos, spiritualism, concept of dead, ancestors, mythological stories and so on. Hindu religion of *Dharma* is based on the theory of rebirth, and various worlds or lives. It is also based on the theory of *karma* and various results thereof. The sin is the root cause of pain, while good deeds lead to progress. These beliefs are more found in the rural society. All aspects of life in rural society are governed by religion and religion provides answer to all superstitions. Rural religion is very strong with a worldly outlook and it covers various aspects of life. Numerous fasts and prayers are much more in practice among the villagers than the urban population.

Various methods of worship—prayers, sacrifice and rituals—are the practical aspects of religion, more practised in the villages. God is treated either as having a form (*sākar*) and without a form (*nirākar*). Prayers are performed to placate gods and goddesses at various places of worship, like temples or in family temples, as a duty in the practice of religion. Sacrifice, as a religious practice, includes giving away of alms (grains, clothes, cash, etc.). Animals are also sacrificed in order to placate gods and goddesses. Rituals, as religious activities, are performed in order to maintain religious and social purity.

The earnest desire of every human being is to be spared of problems in life. He will like to be ever immersed in happiness. The acquisition of spiritual knowledge is necessary for attaining eternal bliss. It will enable him to gain wealth, wisdom, and also to safeguard them. He seeks relief in fasts, prayers, worship, traditional Hindu *Dharma* customs and ceremonies. Man is a sociocultural being and society is both natural and necessary for man. As such all religious activities are subject to social control. Society is a harmonious organization of human relationships and the individuals in a socio-religious group have to live up to the prescribed norms of conduct and the society has to exercise a certain control over its members called social control.

In social control of an individual, the factors notable are the influence exerted through public opinion, coercion, social suggestion, religion, appeal, tolerance or any other method. Influence may be exercised by the society, the family, the church, the state, the club, the school, the trade union, the sermons and preaching in religious congregations (*sateye sang*).

Social control differs from self-control in as much as the latter is from within, while the former is from outside. When an individual controls himself—his impulses—not because of a certain coercion exercised by some other individual or group, but because of his own will and self realization, he is said to have practised self control. It is the individual's own attempt to guide his own behaviour in accordance to some previously developed ideal, goal or purpose. Self control, out of one's own realization, is real and permanent. Man, from birth to death, is undergoing the process of socialization and his behaviour is being controlled in numerous ways. The essence of all religions, the goal of all scriptures and the objective of all aspirations is to remain wedded to virtue adhering to the moral law. The customs regulate the birth and death ceremonies. Diet, dress, manner of speech, marriage, education and a host of other matters are controlled by customs. These customs and procedures become a part of man's life and man gets adjusted to the society. There are various agencies of social control, which exercise regulatory influence over the behaviour of the individual. The formal means of social control are law, education and coercion, which are meant for the society as a whole, but for the individual, with whom we are concerned, informal control can be exercised thus:

BELIEF: Belief is a conviction that a particular thing is true. It is the belief in the existence of an unseen power; the belief in Nemesis, the Goddess of Vengeance; the belief in the existence of hell and heaven and the belief in the immortality of soul.

The belief in the existence of an unseen power leads a man to right action (*Karma*) because he believes that his actions are being watched by an unseen power. The belief in reincarnation keeps the man away from wrongful acts because he believes that in order to have a good birth in next life, he must do good acts in this life. The belief in Nemesis also regulates man's behaviour because he believes that he will be punished for his sins, here and now. The fourth belief in the existence of hell and heaven influences a man to virtuous acts and avoid sins in order to go to heaven or avoid going to hell after death. Heaven is a place full of luxuries, fairies and romance. Hell is a place of terror, miseries and torture. The last belief in the immortality of the soul leads a man to avoid such actions as will cause pain to the souls of the deceased ancestors. Beliefs are powerful influences on human actions. They are vital for human relations. Beliefs may be true or false. They may be founded on factual or faulty evidence, but the question of their validity does not necessarily determine their effectiveness as social/self controls. We act with as much determination from false beliefs as from factually sound ones. Social suggestions (life examples of great men) or ideologies (Fascism, Leninism, etc.) are social control methods for the society as a group, but for the individual, some other means are:

FOLKWAYS: Folkways are the recognized modes of behaviour which arise automatically within a group. They are the behaviour patterns of everyday life, which arise spontaneously and unconsciously in a group. They are, in fact, the habits of the individual, which become common to a group. They are the foundation of the group culture, socially approved with some degree of traditional sanction. The Brāhmins shall not take meat or the Jains shall not take curd, are some of the habits, unconsciously followed.

MORES: Mores are like folkways, with a philosophy of social welfare attached. They have moral sanctions and are thought to be good for social benefit. They relate to the fundamental needs of society more directly than do the folkways. Mores are always moulding human behaviour. They restrain an individual from doing acts contrary to social welfare. In society, there are innumerable mores viz., monogamy, prohibition, endogamy, antislavery, anti-*sati*, etc. Mores control man's behaviour in society to a very large extent.

CUSTOMS: Customs are the long established habits and usage of the people. They are those folkways and mores that have persisted for a very long time and have been passed down from one generation to another. They arise spontaneously and gradually. There is no constituted authority to declare them or to safeguard them. They are accepted by society. They are socially accredited ways of acting. They are socially prescribed modes of behaviour. Their violation brings social disapproval. They are followed because they have been followed in the past. The customs are so powerful that no one can escape their range. They bind men together and regulate social life to a great extent. They are held so sacred that any violation is regarded not only a social crime, but also a sacrilege. In primitive societies, customs were powerful means of social self control but in modern times, their force has decreased.

CEREMONIES: Religion exercises a powerful influence upon man's behaviour in society. Religion is an attitude towards superhuman powers. It is a belief in powers superior to man. It expresses itself in several forms like superstition, animism, totemism, magic, ritualism and fetishism. In every religion beliefs and practices differ, but still religion pervades practically in all societies. Hindu religion assigns great importance to Ceremonies, for example, at the time of birth, marriage and death. Mantras are recited, even without understanding their meaning. Religion makes people benevolent, charitable, forbearing and truthful. All religious ceremonies are observed with a view to make people content with their lot, obedient to their elders and remain wedded to virtue adhering to the moral law.

ART & LITERATURE: Art and literature influence the imagination and exert control on human behaviour. The great epics *Ramayana* and *Mahabharata* are of great social value, and give us information about customs and ceremonies, as they existed in the epic period.

PUBLIC OPINION: Public opinion has a great influence as a means of social control, particularly in village society; where people are known to each other personally. One cannot dare neglect a custom or a ceremony, because of the fear of a social boycott. Ceremonies performed after death of a Hindu, howsoever disliked, are still performed, so that public recognition (opinion) is not degraded.

The greatest contribution of the Hindu philosophy to human thought is its conception of *Dharma*, which governs Hinduism, the system of living, in its social, religious and all other aspects of life. It appears to be synonymous with the western concept of religion, which embraces every kind of supernatural belief, but Hindu *Dharma* is a law of nature, which enables man to attain supreme bliss of life. It is the living experience and leads man to ultimate reality. It is not supernatural belief but a way of rational thinking. It consciously aims at achieving the highest perfection of human life through *Moksha* (salvation, liberation). *Dharma*, according to Mahābhārata, is created for the well being of all creations. All that is free from being harmful to any created being is 'Dharma'. It protects all, preserves all and it is that principle that is capable of preserving the whole universe, being the right order.

According to Dr. R.K. Mukherjee, "*Dharma* like *Brahmā*, in Indian thought, is a notion of many sided import. Metaphysically speaking *Dharma* is *Rita* or the cosmic binding order, the eternal truth holding its sway over universe, in the words of Kautilya's *Arthashāstra*. *Dharma* practice is the law of altruism, complete, balanced and practical, as embodied in the eight fold path and based on the laws of unity, continuity, metapsychosis and transience."

The Hindu social system has insisted on the harmony and cooperation of human beings. In society every individual belongs to a particular group and cultivates a specific nature, which determines human functions. Besides the performance of specific nature duties required by *Dharma*, there are certain functions and duties, which each individual has to perform, irrespective of his nature and class affiliation. Performance and fulfilment of such duties is general and applicable to all human beings, which is called *Manavadharma*. On the other hand, performance of duties prescribed for a class individual is called *Varnadharma*. In addition there is *Svadharma*, which defines the specific law of individual life. The *Gita* is so strong in its insistence upon the law of *Svadharma*. "By his own work (*Svadharma*) a man praised him from whom all things are projected." "Better is death in one's own law (*Svadharma*); for to follow another's law is perilous."

The original devotional movements, among the Hindus, while they sought release from the world (*Moksha*), assumed that as long as one was part of the world, one was part of the Hindu religious organization of life, with its caste, stages and goals. Each had his own *Svadharma*. The life of the householder or the ascetic, the goal of wealth or devotion, were all integrated into the religious organization of life. All were seeking release from *Karma* and transmigration. Devotion tended to be practised in addition to basic rituals and caste rules, although during some of the practices of the devotional movements, such as pilgrimages, caste distinctions, they were sometimes temporarily set aside. *Svadharma* applies to all levels of existence. Therefore, great significance has been given to sacraments in Hindu society, since they are regarded as a part of the religion. Because of this special feature of the sacraments, their sociological significance is constantly increasing.

In the context of Hindu society, sacrament means that activity that helps to achieve purity and as a result of which the complete development of the personality of the individual is made. Sacrament has been adopted as a means in Hindu society and is connected with physical and non physical aspects of man. This helps the sociological progress of the individual and develops in him respect for labour, virtue and duty. Although sacraments exist in all religions as *sunnat* among Muslims and baptism among Christians, but in Hindu society, they are related to the age, occasion and *ashramas* of the individual. Sacrament, according to Hindu view, is that activity, the performance of which makes a matter or person fit for use and develops ability in the person. According to Vir Mitrodaya, sacraments are that ability which arises by the performance of the activities prescribed and sanctioned by the *shastras*. Sacraments are religious activities, which, through mental and intellectual refinements, may develop complete personality of the individual. Sacraments are performed from birth to death. In Hindu religion, there is no provision for natural development of the personality. Sixteen sacraments of the Hindus are connected with some or the other aspects (physical, mental, social or educational) of personality and help their development. There are a number of sacraments, which have been described in the next chapter.

A Hindu, according to *Dharma*, is placed in a broad

classification, from the moment of birth in an environment conducive to his spiritual growth. This presupposes the concepts of *Karma* (actions). This codification of *Dharma* (*Ashrama* system) had universal application. Its thirty general values include truthfulness, compassion, austerity, purity of body and mind, non violence, charity, service to others and devotion to God. It was customary for a child born in a royal family to be educated to develop leadership qualities and the environment and education helped it to develop the necessary skills to rule. The *Ashrama* system (*Brahmacharya*, *Grehastha*, *Vanaprastha* and *Sanyasa*), through which an individual progressed, helped an individual to actualize his potential. This traditional system is no longer in practice.

Hindu customs and ceremonies fall under the category of sacraments viz. personality, material and spiritual development.

CHAPTER II
The Sacraments

THE ACTUAL religious life of a large number of Hindus is deviating from the standards prescribed in the sacred works; but it is also true that many pious and earnest minded are still careful to impose a religious character on every act and circumstance of their domestic life. This is specially true of the Hindu women.

Whatever estimate may be formed of the nature of Indian religious life, it is certain that a genuine Hindu of the old school does not lead two lives. His religion, as it is, can be described as based on his beliefs in his everyday existence. The religion of a Hindu is his constant companion. He never enters a place with the idea of offering common prayer. He visits shrines, with the idea of praying for himself. *Darsan* (reverence) to look at the deity is his main idea in visiting a temple, because he thinks that very view of the deity will confer merit on him. Prostration before the God, repetition of his name or presentation of oblations (offerings) give him the consolation of pleasing the deity. His real religion is an affair of family usage, domestic rituals, and private observance. Interference by the priest (*purohit*) is tolerated. Sacredotism exerts as strong a power over family religion among Hindus, as it does in other religions, like priest in Christianity. Every incident, every circumstance, every operation in a Hindu home life is subject to ecclesiastical law. Each man finds himself cribbed and confined in all his movements, bound and fettered in all he does by the most minute socio-religious customs and traditions. The priests exert a lot of influence, right from birth to death, even after death, in the life of a Hindu. This influence is on the decline, because of the greed and fake priests coming up in this *Kali Yuga*. Howsoever the circumstances have changed, the religion of a Hindu (*Dharma*) is bound up in the bundle of his everyday existence.

As explained earlier, Hindu Sacraments are regarded as part and parcel of *Dharma*. It is the aim of *Dharma* to develop the individual in all aspects. Through the sacraments, the individual can be inspired to achieve the spiritual goals and merit for his day to day life. The person performing the sacraments is not only engrossed in the worldly life, but also establishes a harmony between physical things and spiritual aspirations. The form and number of sacraments have been a matter of great differentiation. According to *Greha Sutra*, the number of sacraments is 11; *Gaytam Dharma Sutra* numbers the sacraments as 40; *Vaikhanasa* numbers them as 18; *Smriti Chandrikā* mentions the number of sacraments as 16. In ancient collection of domestic rules (Greha *Sutras*) and in the Code of Manu, twelve purificatory rites called *Sanskaras* (Sacraments) were prescribed for the purification of a man's whole nature viz.: body, soul and spirit from the taint transmitted through the womb of an earthly mother.

The more important sacraments are as follows:

1. *Garbhadana* or *Garbha-Lambhana*: Impregnation. This is the first sacrament, which followed immediately on every matrimonial union. In ancient times, no bridegroom approached the bride till the fourth night, after the completion of the marriage ceremony. The present interval of two, three or four years, is quite unsupported by ancient *Sutras*. This first rite was sometimes called *Chaturthi Karma*. During the previous day, the bride and the bridegroom, after ablutions purified their bodies, and before approaching his wife, which act might bring another human being into the world, the bridegroom repeated two *mantras* (*R'Gveda* X. 186): "Let all pervading Vishnu prepare her womb; let the

creator shape the forms; let Prajapati be the impregnator; let the creator give the embryo." This sacrament, in modern times, is a physical act and has lost its religious sanctity.

2. *Pumsavana*: *Punsavan*: The Impregnation Rite: This rite was followed after three months. This rite was performed for getting a handsome strong male child (son). According to Vedic texts, the husband prayed, by the side of his wife, that she might give birth to a son. In this sacrament wife used to observe fast and wear new clothes. A son is fancifully said to mean one who delivers a parent from a hell called Put. The well being of the parent's soul, after death, is believed to depend on the proper performance of the *Shraddha* ceremonies by a son, and that the partition of the family inheritance is by law made dependent on the due celebration of such rites. This is the reason why there is a craving for a son, rather than a daughter. A son is to every Hindu, the first and last of all necessary wishes. With the introduction of Family Planning and the new laws of Hindu inheritance, the craving for a son, has diminished; but still its importance has not been lost. Aitareya-Brāhmana of the *R'Gveda* VII.3.13 says, "When a father sees the face of a living son, he pays a debt in him, and gains immortality. The pleasure, which a father has in his son, exceeds all other enjoyments. His wife is a friend, his daughter an object of compassion, his son shines as his light in the highest world." Manu says, "A man is perfect when he consists of three: himself, his wife and his son." (VII.3) Yajnavalkya says, "Immortality in future worlds and heavenly bliss are obtained by means of sons, grandsons and great grandsons."

A further supplementary rite *Anavalopna* (*Anavalobhana*) for the prevention of miscarriage was customary in some localities. It was performed by sprinkling the juice of a stalk of *Durba* grass in the wife's right nostril, with the repetition of certain *mantras*. This rite is no longer in practice. The importance of having a male child, however diminished, still lies in his exclusive right of offering flames to the pyre of his parents.

3. *Seemantonnyan* or Hair Parting: This sacrament is performed in the fourth month of pregnancy. It starts with the oblation to fire, with repetition of the Vedic texts (*Atharva Veda* VII.17.1 *Rigveda* III.59.1; V.25; II 32.4-5). The woman then performed her ablutions in pure water; fragrant oil was poured on her head and a line or parting (*Simanta*) was drawn three times through her hair from the forehead upwards with three stalks of *Kusa* grass bound together. Three sacred words called *vyahritis* (*Bhur, Bhavar, Svar*) and the hallowed syllable OM (AUM) uttered during each operation. Certain medicines, having purifying efficacy for the remaining period of gestation, were also given. Musical entertainment and cheering took place, thought essential for the proper development of the unborn child. The idea was that the body of the mother should be consecrated and protected from evil influences at the critical period of gestation. This rite is only performed for the first pregnancy.

4. *Jatā Karman* or Birth Ceremony: This *sanskara* (sacrament) is performed after the birth of the infant and before the severing of the umbilical cord, by the father. Honey and *ghee* (clarified butter) mixed together, stirred by a golden rod or spoon, a small portion of the mixture is introduced into the mouth of the new born infant. This rite symbolized good fortune. Certain texts were repeated (R'G*veda* II.21.6; III.36.10) with the prayer: "O long lived one, may you live a hundred years in this world, protected by the Gods." Both the ears of the infant were then touched with the golden rod repeating the prayer, "May Sāvitri, May Saraswati, May the Asvins, grant thee wisdom." Lastly, rubbing the shoulders, the prayer uttered is, "Become firm as a rock, sharp as an axe, pure as gold; thou art the *Veda* called a son, live thou a hundred years. May Indra bestow on thee his best treasures."

5. *Nām Karan* (*Nām Karana* - Name giving): Among the Hindus, giving a name, is a solemn religious ceremony, fraught with important consequences in its bearing on the future prospects of the infant. Asvalayasa laid down the rules based on the sound and meaning in name giving. The name of the boy should be in two, four or even syllables and have a soft consonant for the first letter and a semi vowel in the middle e.g. . Bhadra, Deva etc. Sarman (prosperity) for Brāhmins and Varman for *kshatriyas*; Gupta (protected) for *Vaishyas* and Dāsa (Slave) for *Sudras* were prescribed. The female names were required to be agreeable, soft, clear, captivating, auspicious and ending in long vowels. This sacrament is performed on the 10th or 11th day of the birth of the child. On this occasion, food is given to the Brahmin etc. According to Manu, *Nām Karan* of each caste should be made in a different way

6. *Nishkramana* (Carrying Out). In this sacrament, the child is taken out of the house for the first time and is made to have a "*Darshan*' of the Sun. This sacrament is performed by the parents after four months of the birth of the child. The prayer made at the occasion is: "That 'eye like' luminary, the cause of blessings to the Gods (or placed in the sky by the Gods), rises in the East; may we behold it for a hundred years." "May we hear, may we speak, may we be free from poverty for a hundred years and more." (R'*Gveda* VII.66.16; Vaj - Samhita XXXVI.24)

7. *Anna Prasana* (Food Giving): This is a very popular and important sacrament, performed in the sixth month of the birth of the child. The child, carried by the father, is placed between gathered relatives and friends. The family priest offers prayers for the welfare of the child. The invitees present gifts. Now that the child is fit to consume solid food, the father of the child or any other member of the family, gives food, usually rice cooked in milk (*Kheer*), to the child. In Bengal, this preparation is called *Pias*. After this, the child

can consume solid food. In Bengal, this *sanskar* is performed in the seventh month for the girls and in the eighth month for boys.

8. *Choodā Karan* (Tonsure, Shaving, Cutting of the hair): The first tonsure of a child is an important rite, but it is known by various names and celebrated in various ways by different castes in different localities. In the southwest, it is known as the *Jhand* and elsewhere as the *Mundan* or *Bhaddan*. If the mother had made a vow prior to the birth of the child to observe the rite at a certain shrine or temple, it is duly carried out there; otherwise it may be done at home. An auspicious hour should be fixed by a Brahmin, or the rite should be performed on the marriage of a near kinsman, or on the *Baisakhi* or *Dussehra*. It is unlucky to shave a child's head, until this rite has been performed. According to Vedic texts, the performance of this sacrament increases happiness, good fortune and enthusiasm. This sacrament can be performed in between the end of the first and the third year of the birth of the child, or as the child cuts his teeth. Sometimes the rite is repeated once or twice.

The observance of this sanskār (rite) is essentially a domestic usage, varying in the details according to the ancestral custom of the caste, section or even family. Sometimes women vow that child's hair shall never be cut. Among Sikhs, the rite is not very common and a girl's hair is never cut. Among Sikhs, the rite is not very common and if observed, the hair is cut, when the child is only two or three months old. In well-to-do families, the rite is the occasion for a feast to Brāhmins, otherwise they play no part in this sacrament. The menials receive fees, and the brotherhood is regaled with sweets at the first tonsure, after which *bodi* or tuft of hair is allowed to grow, but it is more usual to let the *bodi* grow after the marriage of a near kinsman.

This sacrament also called *Caula*, *Cuda-Karma*,

Kesanta or *Kshaura*, is said to have a purificatory effect on the whole character of the child, when performed for the first time. According to Asvalayana, the child was to be placed on the lap of its mother to the west of the sacred fire. The father was to take up his station to the south of the mother, holding in his hand twenty one stalks of *Kusa* grass. He has to sprinkle the head of the child three times with a mixture of warm water, butter and curd. He has to insert three stalks of *Kusa* grass seven times into the child's hair on the right side, saying: "O Divine grass, protect him." Then the hair is cut with recitation of various texts.

9. *Karna Bheda* (Ear Boring): In this sacrament, the ears of the child are pierced through for the first time. This rite is treated by some as a distinct religious rite, and has to take place after tonsure at three or five years of age. This is no longer a common rite. *Greh Sutras* do not mention this rite. Paraskara made it a sanskar, but not so Asvalayana or Gobhila. The boy was fed with honey or something sweet, and was made to sit with the face towards the east. Then two perforations were made in his right ear and a particular hymn from the last hymn of the *Sama Veda* is recited. "Let us hear what is good with the ears, let us see what is good with the eyes." A similar operation is then performed on the left ear, except that three perforations are made and a different *mantra* from the R'*Gveda* (VI. 75-3) recited. "This bowstring drawn tight upon the bow and leading to success in battle, repeatedly approaches the ear, as if embracing its friends and wishing to say something agreeable, just as a woman makes a murmuring sound, in her husband's ear." This sacrament is performed for enabling the child to wear ornaments, as we see on the ears of the rajas, maharajas and wealthy *vaish* persons.

10. *Upānayana* (Initiation): Upānayana simply means leading or bringing a boy to his *guru* or spiritual preceptor. In real fact, until the boy was so brought, he could not be

invested with the sacred thread, and until he was so invested he could not be reckoned among the "twice borns" (*Dvija*). So a sacrament called *Vidyarambha* (start of education) was observed which was necessary to start the education of the child. In this sanskār, the child has to first take a bath and then taken to the *guru* for learning the letters. After this initiation comes the very important sacrament of Upanayāna, which is essential to determine the social status of the individual. This is performed at the age of eight or may be deferred till sixteen. It is only when a boy has been invested with the sacred thread, he has a right to the title *Dvija* (twice born). The Brahmins, *Kshatriyas* and *Vaishyas* are called *Dvijas*, because they undergo the sacrament of initiation. According to Hindu *Dharma Shastras*, a man is a *shudra* by birth, but after initiation, he becomes a *Dvija*. Initiation sacrament is not allowed for *shudras;* so all Hindus are divided into two broad categories *Dvijas* and *Shudras*. It is only after initiation, that a person could be permitted to use a single prayer, or repeat the *Vedas* or engage in any single religious service or sacrificial rite. Any ceremonial observance is ineffectual, unless the thread (*Janeo*) is worn. A Brāhmin, before initiation is called a *Vipra*, and after initiation, he becomes qualified to learn the *Veda* (Brahma) by heart. This ancient belief in birth as a *Shudra*, or a *Vipra*, before thread ceremony, is no longer a Brāhmin by birth and so on. At the present day, it is not always that the *Janeo* is worn by the higher castes; while on the other hand, the so called *Shudra* castes not infrequently wear it.

The form of the sacred thread (*Janeo*) varies in every caste group or sect. These forms are:

1. *Brahmgandh*: (a) With 5 knots for the higher grades of Brāhmins.
   (b) With 3 knots or the lower grades of Brāhmin
2. *Vishnugandh*: With one knot for all other castes.

If a Brāhmin wishes to become learned in the *Vedas*, he should wear the *Janeo* at the age of five years; if a *Kshatriya* wishes to gain strength, he should wear it at six, and for a *Vaishya*, if he desires success, he should wear the *Janeo* in the eighth year of age. (Manu Smriti Chapter II.36 and 37).

Making of the *Janeo*

The cotton is purchased on the 13th day after the new moon in August-September. It is spun into thread by Brahmin girls or by married women whose husband is alive, never by a widow. The cotton should be picked up from the field, free from filth. A *Janeo* may consist of one or two Agras. There are three lines on the fingers. The Brahmins should wind the single thread over the upper line 96 times, the *Kshatriyas* over the central line 86 times and the *Vaishyas* over the lower line for 76 times. The thread is then made into three folds and twisted on a *Kath* (a special tool used in preparing the *Janeo*). It is then folded in three folds a second time, so that there are now nine threads in the cord. To make an *Agra*, it is again folded thrice making 27 threads in each *Agra*. The number of knots in an *Agra* depends on the number of famous ancestors in each *gotra*. One *Agra* is allowed to a Brāhmin in the *Brahmchari* or disciplinary stage, the second being added when he reaches the second ashram *Grehsthashram* (house holder state). The first thread should be twisted from right to left, the second from left to right and so on. The second *Agra* is made in the same way and when two are worn, they should be knotted together by three or five knots. Rituals provide specific duration and material for different type of *Janeos* for different castes (*varna*):

Brāhmin	Cotton	96 *chappas*	8th-16th yr age
Kshatriya	Hemp	95 *chappas*	11th-22nd yr age
Vaishye	Wool	94 *chappas*	12th-24th yr age

(A *chappa* is four finger's breadth)

Between the above periods, a *Janeo* may be worn at any time, but if the Brahmin desires learning *Veda*s or a *Kshatriya* wish strength, then the age is earlier, as described earlier. The rules as to material are not now observed at all strictly, but the rule regarding the length of the sacred thread is generally followed.

The Ceremony: On an auspicious day and at auspicious time, the boy's head is shaved, saving the middle tuft (*bodi*). After bath, he is seated on the skin of an animal (deer, sheep or goat, according to caste). The *guru* makes the boy sit on his left side, making him promise to obey the orders he will receive, covers both their hands with a long cloth; amidst the beating of drums and sounding of conches, the guru whispers in the right ear of the boy a *mantra*, which is never revealed to others. The boy then goes to his mother and begs alms and later from all other assembled women. These alms consisting of money, rice, wheat, small rings of silver or gold, etc. are then given to the *guru* who then puts the *Janeo* on the boy. During the operation, holy water is sprinkled with a tuft of grass and *Gayatri mantra* is recited. Now for the first time, the boy is taught to repeat that remarkable Vedic prayer for illumination called Savitri, or Gayatri from R'G*veda* III. 62.10, thus translatable: "Let us meditate on that excellent glory of the divine vivifier, may He illuminate our understandings." (that most ancient of all Aryan prayers, which was first uttered more than three thousand years ago, and which still rises day by day towards heaven, incessantly ejaculated by millions of our nationals). He is taught to pronounce the sacred syllable 'OM' (AUM), the names of the seven worlds (*Bhur*, *Bhuvar*, *Svar*, etc.) and other Vedic texts. The whole process of teachings from Manu, Sanskrit books, law books, enjoining abstinence from injury to others, unselfishness, the practice of truth, honesty, chastity and self control, starts after this *Janeo* ceremony.

Modes of Wearing the *Janeo*: The *Janeo* is ordinarily worn over the left shoulder, across the back and chest, and under the right shoulder but during worship it is held differently. While worshipping the gods, the *Janeo* is worn on the left shoulder, but is held across the palm under the thumb of the left hand; the right hand is kept over it forward. In the worship of ancestors (*Pitris*), the *Janeo* is worn on the right shoulder, and the libation of water made with the finders of the right hand, the palm being kept above them, so as to pour the water to the left. In worshipping the *Rishis* the *Janeo* is placed round the neck and allowed to fall like a necklace. The thread ceremony (*Janeo*), as prescribed in the Vedic text books and scriptures, is no longer in practice in the modern society of the Hindus. *Kashatriyas* and *Vaishyas* hardly wear the Janeo in any part of India. Even the Brāhmins do not wear it generally. In Southern India and in Bengal, however, the Brāhmins perform this sacrament religiously and they can be recognized by the *Janeo* on their body. Howsoever modernized, this ceremony is still the second most sacred ceremony among the Hindus, next to the sanskar of marriage. According to Manu, a Brāhmin's life in ancient times was to be divided into the four stages, called *Ashrams* viz.: *Brahmachari* (student), *Grehastha* (household), *Vanprastha* (anchorite) and *Sanyas* or *Bhikshu* (religious mendicant or abandoner of all worldly concerns). Hence immediately after the initiation ceremony, he had to leave the parent's house and reside with a religious preceptor for several years as an unmarried student, till he had acquired a good knowledge of the *Vedas*. He was then to perform the next *sanskāra Samavartana* (Return). This was formally a solemn religious observance in which prayers were recited, ablutions performed, and gifts given to the spiritual teacher. After this he could return to his father's house and start *Grehsth* life, as a married person.

CHAPTER III
Marriage

AFTER SAMAVARTANA (return), the Hindu enters *grehasth*, that is married life. Custom of marriage is the most widespread institution of human society. Since the prehistoric period up to the present age marriage has remained the backbone of human civilization. Therefore, the institution of marriage occupies a very important place in human society. It is an institution that admits men and women to family life. It is a stable relationship in which a man and a woman are socially permitted to have children implying the right to sexual relations. In India, since ancient times, marriage has been regarded as a sacrament and is obligatory on all the "twice borns" (*Dwija*) except those who desire to adopt the life of a *Brahmachari* of professed religious studentship or other asceticism.

Marriage is, however, by Hindu Law a civil contract, carrying with it serious obligations. Among Hindus, marriage is a religious duty. It is neither a social contract nor its ultimate aim is enjoyment or procreation of children. It is essential for every Hindu, so he may repay his social and parental debts. Among Hindus, marriage is a holy union between a man and a woman for begetting a son, necessary for salvation and/or religious duties. Hindu's marriage is not dissolved after the death of any one of the partners. Marriage is so important and indispensable among Hindus that a person, who does not marry is disdained. This is the most important of all *sanskaras* (sacraments). Throughout the ages, for which literary tradition is available, an Indian marriage has been highly thought of. (P.V. Kane:

History of Dharmashastras Vol. II, Part I: 1941). Mazumdar HT (Grammar of Sociology) defines marriage as "a socially sanctioned union of male and female, or as a secondary institution devised by society to sanction the union and mating of male and female, for purposes of (a) establishing household (b) entering into sex relations (c) procreating and (d) providing care for the off spring".

Marriage is a sacred duty among Hindus, a duty that every parent must perform for his children, otherwise they owe him no reverence. A family with a daughter unmarried after the age of puberty is considered to labour under the displeasure of gods. No member of the other sex considers himself respectable after the age of puberty till he is married. It is the duty of his parents or elder brothers to have him suitably married; and if they do not do so, he reproaches them with his degraded condition. According to Manu, a man who does not marry, never receives worship after death. His happiness in the next world depends upon a continuous line of male descendants, who make periodical offerings for the peace of his soul.

"To be mothers, women created, and to be fathers, men. Therefore, the Vedas ordain that *dharma* must be practised by man together with his wife." In all religious ceremonies, the husband and wife are made to sit side by side, for example, in a *yajna* or at the marriage ceremony of the children. Once Brahma was to perform a *puja* and his wife, Saraswati, was late to come. Therefore, Brahma had to perform an immediate marriage with Savitri so that she could sit by his side for the performance of the yajna. Apart from this, without marriage a man cannot enter into the *Grihasthashram*. Mahabharata has clearly indicated that an unmarried girl cannot enter heaven, despite all religious practices. Similarly, a man shall remain in various painful stages, unless death ceremonies are not properly observed by his male descendants. According to Hindu scriptures, by entering Grihasthashram through marriage a man can attain fullest development of life in all spheres like dharma (religious uplift), *arth* (wealth), *kama* (sexual pleasure) and *moksha* (liberation from earthly bondages). Thus, in Hindu marriage, sex is secondary and Dharma is primary. Hindu philosophy recognizes the spiritual ideal of marriage. The Hindus regard marriage relation as indissoluble.

Forms of marriage

1. Polyandry: In this one wife is regarded as the wife of all brothers, who have sexual relation with her. Among the Todas, this custom still exists. In some cases, the husbands may not be brothers but cohabitors.

2. Polygyny: In this system, one man has two or more wives at a time. It is popularly called polygamy. Whereas this is common among the Muslims in India, among Hindus it existed when the chieftains and Rajahs ruled their states. However, with the change in the Hindu Law, polygamy has become a crime under the Hindu Marriage Act, 1955.

3. Monogamy: One man, one wife. This is the leading form of marriage. It produces the highest type of affection and sincere devotion. The children are well looked after.

4. Companionate Marriage: This is the marriage of two persons on the understanding that as long as there are no children, the marriage may be dissolved simply by mutual consent. This system is non existent now.

5. Experimental Marriage: Experimental marriages to find out the compatibility of the two people before they settle down to a life of permanent union, is fine in the laboratory, and not in marriage.

Kinds of Marriage

Eight kinds of marriage have been recognized in Hindu Law books.

1. Brahma *vivah* (marriage): The gift of a daughter,

clothed only with a single robe, to a man learned in the Vedas, who her father voluntarily invites and respectfully receives, is the nuptial, called Brahma. After the bride and the bridegroom have undergone thorough education in *Brahmacharya Ashrama* and when both are in agreement, the father of the bride gives his daughter to the bridegroom, as a gift. Usually ornaments accompany her, according to one's capacity. According to Kautilaya, "The giving in marriage maiden well adorned is called Brahma marriage." This ceremony was formerly peculiar to the Brahmins, but is now performed by all castes of Hindus.

2. *Daiva* Vivah: In this form of marriage, the father gives his daughter along with ornaments to a priest, who duly officiated at a sacrifice (Yajna) during the course of its performance. Such marriages were more frequent in those times, when yajna was an essential part of the daily activities of Hindus.

3. *Arsha* Vivah: In this kind of marriage, the bridegroom offered a cow and a bull to the father of the bride, and the latter gave his daughter in marriage. This taking of the cow and the bull was a religious requirement, as a token of gratitude to the man, who offered his daughter to the groom to enable him to fulfil the obligations of Grihasthashram.

4. *Prajapatya* Vivah: The joint performance of sacred duties by man and a woman is known as Prajapatya marriage. According to Swami Dayanand Saraswati, the founder of Arya Samaj, the father gives his daughter to the bridegroom, by addressing the couple with the mantras, "May both of you perform together your dharma." This kind of marriage is similar to Brahma vivah, which may be the origin of Prajapatya vivah.

5. *Asura* Vivah: This is a kind of marriage where the bridegroom has to pay the price to the father or kinsmen of the bride. The bridegroom fixes the price according to the

status of the bride's family. This form of marriage is more popular amongst low caste Hindus. This kind of marriage is common among the tribes in India.

6. *Gandharva* Vivah: Mutual love and consent between bride and the bridegroom, are the only conditions to bring about such a marriage. It is a voluntary union of a maiden with her lover. Parents and kinsmen have nothing to do in such marriages. Sexual intercourse before marriage may occur between the couple. It is not regarded as a disqualification for their subsequent marriage. Kama Sutra regards this marriage as an ideal one. Hindu mythology literature abounds in such type of marriages. For example, of Dushyant and Shakuntala; Daksheya and Prajapati, Bhima with Hidimba; Arjuna with a servant maid, Kamdeva and Rati, Kach and Devyani, and many more described in Sukh Sagar.

Another form of marriage, which existed in ancient times, was one by *Swaymbara*. It was more or less the selection of a hero as a bridegroom. The royalty of olden times wanted to select a brave and righteous person. So invitations were sent to the nearby princes and the chieftains in different kingdoms. The bride was given the choice to select one from the gathered ones whom she selected by putting a garland round his neck and the marriage was complete. The marriage of Nala and Damayanti happened this way. In the marriage between Prithviraj and Sanyukta, the bride had put a garland round the neck of a statue of Prithviraj. In certain cases, a test was conducted and the winner was garlanded as the bridegroom. This system was followed in Ramayana when Rama pulled the string of Śiva's bow to marry Sita or in Mahābhārata, where Arjuna shot through the eye of the revolving fish on the top of a pole to marry Draupadi. Swaymbara has not been included in the eight forms of classical/ traditional marriages, but has been recognized as a form of Gandharva marriage. In this type of marriage, it is also possible that, at a time when the father permitted his daughter to choose her husband, love and courtship might have been the order of the day. In such cases, a passionate couple might have entered into a union without going through the religio-legal formalities. This could occur more frequently during wars. It is possible that later on, the union was legalized through a proper ceremony, therefore it was recognized as an approved form.

7. *Rakshasa* Vivah: This was a marriage by capture. Primitive tribes regarded women as prizes of war, part of the plunder in a fair fight. This form was common in many other ancient civilizations. It appealed to the warrior instinct of the *Kshatriya*, and was sometimes practised by them. The origin of this form of marriage probably lay among the non-Aryans. Hindu scriptures describe this form of marriage as forcible abduction of a maiden from her home, while she cries and weeps, after her kinsmen have been slain or wounded and their house broken. Women, thus, caused many fights and battles in ancient times.

8. *Paishacha* Vivah: This was the worst form of all types of marriages. In this the bride was abducted, but not in a fair fight with her tribe. She was molested or stolen, when she and her relatives were asleep, or in a state of intoxication during a tribal festival. This form is universally condemned. The inclusion of this form of marriage in Hindu Sutras, can only be justified on the ground that it was so prevalent among the primitive tribes that the Sutras could not have avoided its inclusion. By recognition of this form, the only advantage was that the children could be regarded as legitimate.

According to Kautilya, "Of these eight forms of marriage, only the first four (Brahma, Daiva, Arsha and Prajapatya) are ancestral customs of old and are valid on their being approved by the father. The rest, for it is that they receive money, the money paid by the bridegroom for their daughter. In case of absence by death of either the father or the mother, the survivor will receive the money. If both of them are dead, the maiden herself shall receive it. Any kind of marriage is approvable, provided it pleases all those that are concerned with it." All these forms of marriage are valid, only if it has been approved by the father.

Hindu Marriage Act of 1955

The Hindu marriage Act, 1955 has now regulated the.marriage among Hindus. Section 5 of the Act lays down: "A marriage may be solemnized between any two Hindus, if the following conditions are satisfied:

(i) Neither part has a spouse living at the time of marriage.

(ii) Neither party is an idiot or a lunatic at the time of the marriage.

(iii) The bridegroom has completed the age of eighteen years and the bride the age of fifteen years respectively.

(iv) The parties are not within the degrees of prohibited relationship, unless the custom or usage governing each of them permits of a marriage between the two.

(v) The parties are not *sapindas* of each other, unless the custom or usage governing each of them, permits of a marriage between the two.

(vi) Where the bride has not completed the age of eighteen years, the consent of her guardians in marriage, if any, has been obtained for the marriage.

Exogamy

The Hindus are the only civilized people, whose marriage laws are based on the principle of exogamy. Under the usage and custom of the Hindus, no two persons tracing their common ascendancy through their father within five degrees of ascendancy, can at all marry among themselves. While on the mother's side, the restriction extends up to third degree. From the highest Brahmins to the rudest tribes of the Nilgiri hills and Assam, the system of exogamy is prevalent. Among the Brahmins and Vaishyas, the name of the exogamous unit is known as *Gotra*. Among the Rajputs, the name is Nukh, while among the lower castes in Northern India, it is Kul. In southern India, it is called Intiperu or Hilai or Bedhul or Bali. Males and females having the same Gotra do not marry, according to *Grihasutras* and Dharmashastras. So far as the maternal side is concerned, the problem of exogamy is dealt with side *sapinda*. Therefore, no man can marry a woman, who is sapinda on his mother's side.

"These exogamous taboos are designed as restrictions of free marital relationship. Their psychological origin lies in the horror of incest and the consequent incest taboo, which aims at preventing sex relations between parents and offspring, and between brothers and sisters." (P.N. Prabhu). P.V. Kane has assigned two reasons to this system: (i) if near relatives marry, their defects are transmitted with aggravation to their offspring and (ii) the fear that there may be clandestine love affairs and consequent loss of morals.

Child Marriage

The Vedic texts, the *R'gveda* do not make any clear mention about the suitable age of boys and girls. Vedic texts imply grown up brides. In the earlier *greha* and dharma sutras, the bride was a grown up maiden; but in the later sutras it is stated that the bride should not have reached the age of puberty. The custom of child marriages became the rule around the 2nd century AD; this trend became pronounced between 2nd to 4th century AD, after which it became the rule.

In the period of Dharmashāstras, child marriage received much encouragement. According to Brahma Purana, a girl after the age of 4 years could be married at any time. Child marriage is prohibited under the existing Hindu Law (Hindu Marriage Act 1955).

Child marriage had certain merits. By living together from a very early age, harmony was brought into the nature of the husband and the wife. Early marriage was a check on immorality and corruption. Responsibility entrusted early in life developed self dependability and children at an early age enabled the parents to fulfil their social responsibilities. However, there were more demerits in child marriage than its merits. These included maternal mortality, infant mortality, over population, loss of higher education of parents, debilitated and sick women, increase in the number of child widows, weak and unhealthy children; early increase of duties and responsibilities of the husband resulted in lack of wisdom and curbed individual freedom.

To check the custom of child marriage in India as many as six Acts have been passed since 1860, but these Acts failed to achieve the desired results. In the year 1954 Special Marriage Act was passed, which fixed the marriageable age of the boys as 21 and those of the girls 18 years. Any person who violated this age bar was punishable under the Act. Finally, the Hindu Marriage Act was passed in 1955, according to which, a marriage will be valid only if the boy and the girl have attained the age of 18 years and 15 years respectively.

Widow Marriage

There are many references of widow marriage in ancient Indian literature. In the Vedic age, widow marriages were not prohibited. According to Nārad Purāna, there are three types of widow marriages: (i) for a woman, who has been married, but no cohabitation has taken place with her husband; (ii)a woman who after leaving her first husband, returns to him after leaving her second husband and (iii) a woman, who after the death of her husband, has been given

Indian Marriage

to any sapinda. R'gveda prescribes that the widow should give up thinking of the deceased husband and should accept the offer of the person who wants to marry her.

According to Yaska's Nirukta: "The custom of widow marrying the brother-in-law of the deceased husband, was general, when the dead body of the deceased husband, was going to be cremated, the dead man's brother seized the widow with the following verse:

'Arise, woman, than art lying by one, whose life is gone, come to the world of the living, away from the husband, and become the wife of him, who grasps thy hand, woos thee as a lover.'"

Vashishtha and Kautilya in *Arthashāstra* have

permitted widow marriage. During the Epic period, there was no restriction or check on the marriage of widows. According to Manu Smṛiti, "those women who do not have sexual intercourse with their first husband can remarry". In the middle ages, Chandragupta Vikramāditya had married the wife of his deceased brother. Vashishta and Prashar Smriti have been more liberal in their approach: "if the husband disappears, dies, becomes a saint, becomes impotent or becomes a debauch, then the woman concerned can remarry".

Still, from the beginning of 10th to 11th century AD, widow marriages were rather universally prohibited. As long as the *sati* custom continued to be prevalent, the condition of the widows in the Hindu society was deplorable. Forcible widowhood led to illicit sexual connections, abduction, kidnapping, prostitution and illegitimate children. Therefore, no woman should be forced to lead a life of widowhood against her wishes. Motherhood is the aim of every woman and therefore child widows and widows without children should be allowed to remarry. From the humanitarian point of view, for womanhood, for the liberation of child widows and as a check on immorality widows should be allowed to remarry.

Validity of widow's remarriage was legalized by The Hindu Widow Remarriage Act of 1856. Besides, Hindu Succession Act, 1956 and Hindu Marriage Act, 1955, also contain provisions regarding remarriage of the widows.

Divorce

Divorce is alien to Hindu point of view. Hindus consider marriage a sacrament, which is regarded unbreakable throughout one's life. There is no reference to divorce in the whole of Vedic literature, and in Manu Smriti. Kautilya's Arthashastra, however, says, "If there is mutual enjoy or jealousy between the wife and the husband, then they can leave each other; however, consent of both is necessary for this." These restrictions were only in accordance with contemporary circumstances and conditions. Present age believes in providing equal opportunities to each person for his or her development. Hence in the Special Marriage Act 1954, an amendment to 1872 Act was passed, mainly in the interest of those persons, who solemnize marriage, not as a religious sacrament, but in civil court. The Hindu Marriage Act 1955 accorded validity to the provisions of divorce. Under this Act, both husband and the wife can seek divorce. However, no application for divorce can be submitted within three years of marriage. Moreover, the divorced person cannot remarry within one year of getting the divorce.

The Marriage Ceremony

The marriage ceremony has various stages: selection of bride and the bridegroom; betrothal, marriage and after-marriage ceremonies.

Selection of the Couple

The selection of the bride and bridegroom is generally made by the parents or the elders. They, being experienced men, can better evaluate the merits of the partners. The boy and the girl, being young, are raw hands and can be led to more transitory, rather than permanent valuable considerations. Love marriage is generally disliked. This system of selection by the parents has been criticized because it has come to light that in many cases, parents marry their son or daughter to one who is not a suitable match on biological or psychological grounds, but whose status and wealth would add greatly to their prestige. It is, therefore, desirable that the boy and the girl should be consulted, emphasizing on them the reasons for the selection by the parents. Today the young boys and girls have a terrifying desire of a perfect marriage and a new marriage must not be hampered by old attitudes. In their would-be partner, the youngsters want beautiful facial characteristics, unmitigated love, devotion and fidelity and also camaraderie and complete self expression. They fail to see the reality of marriage and when they fail, they put the blame on the parents instead of upon the excessive and naive demands they make on the marriage. The parents are morally bound to find mates for their children and the children are obliged to accept the parental choice. The marriage among Hindus is considered a union between two families rather than between two young people. However two considerations are always there that the mates must be chosen outside the family and must be within the caste. However, western culture has come heavy upon the youngsters and traditional Hindu customs are ignored in the modern age.

In the past, the selection of the couple was based on Shastric ideas and a glimpse into the same may be interesting. The guardians of the girl should not only see the boy's body, but also consider his conduct, family means, education and repute. He should choose one whose age is more than the girl, but not much more (as treble her age). The boy should be sound in body and in mind and his family should be free from hereditary diseases. He should not live too far away, nor be constantly engaged in war (no longer applicable) nor an ascetic, and apart from these general considerations, he should have the following particularized qualifications:

Broad or deep: chest, face and forehead, his naval, voice and inherent power.

Short: throat, back, male organ and legs.

Fine: hair, nails, teeth, flesh and the joints of the fingers.

Long: the distance between the eyebrows and his breasts, his arms, his nostrils and his chin.

Red: his palate and tongue, the soles of his feet and the palms of his hands, and both corners of each eye.

On the other hand, the girl should be *aspinda,* that is, not related to the boy within the following degrees.

She should not be of the same Gotra as the boy. She should not have been born in the *Mangal Ras* (house of mars); if so the boy selected should also be a *mangalik.*

The girl should be a virgin, beautiful, young and free from disease. She should also have a brother, for otherwise, according to the marriage contract, her first born son would have to be given to her father, in order that he might become his maternal grandfather's heir.

Various other qualifications are prescribed. Health, good repute, a swan like gait, fine teeth and hair, delicate limbs and red soled feet without prominent joints. Her fingers and toes should be separated, and the palm of her hand shaped like a lotus for luck. Her shape should be fish-like, and on the soles of her feet there should be the marks of a good and barley corns. Her knees should be round, her legs free from hair, her forehead broad and prominent, the naval deep, with three deep wrinkles in the abdomen, the nipples round and hard, the throat like a lion, the lips as red, the voice soft like a cuckoo's, the nostrils evenly matched, and the eyes like lotus. Lastly, her little toes should not touch the ground lest she becomes a widow, the second toe should not project beyond the big toe, lest her character be lost, and her legs should not be long and thin, for that too, is an omen of widowhood. Hair on the legs presages misfortune, and a prominent abdomen lasting sickness and sterility. Her eyes should not be reddish brown, nor like those of a cat, for the latter denote easy virtue. Hair on the nipples will bring misfortune on her husband. Dry hair and everted lips show a quarrelsome temper, and so on. These qualifications are based on Shāstric laws and astrological readings.

These qualifications in a boy and a girl, are, no doubt, of great value, but with the change in the circumstances and the modern thinking of the boys and the girls, these are ignored.

The Betrothal

When the selection of the boy for a bridegroom and of the girl for the bride have been investigated and the betrothal decided on, an auspicious day is fixed for its celebration, which should not take place in the month of Posh (December), *Kartik* (October) or *Chetra* (March), when Venus and Jupiter are on the wane, during the *shhrādas*, annual or general, interrelated months or when the Venus and the Jupiter are in the same rāsa and soon. Sundays, Tuesdays and Saturdays, are also to be avoided. The ideal time for betrothal is during the following *Nakshatras* (asterisms): *Phālgun* (January-February), *Bhādrapada* (August-September) and June-August.

On the day, appointed for the rite, the boy's party goes to the girl's house and both parties are seated, while Brahmins recite the *Mangla Charan* (benedictory prayer) and Shri Ganesh is worshipped, kept in a brass dish. Rice is sprinkled on Ganesh and the boy's party. Sometimes red coloured water is also sprinkled over them. The girl's guardian (the father, paternal grandfather, brother, one of the same family and lastly the mother) then announces that the girl, daughter of so and so, is *dan* (gift) by word of mouth, and is the essence of the betrothal contract. It is now irrevocable, and there is a very strong feeling against breaking it. When once the promise has passed the lips of the girl's guardian, it can only be withdrawn for grave causes. Then a *janeo* (sacred thread), fruits, flowers and some clothes are given to the boy by the girl's guardian. The girl's Brahmin applies *tilak* to the boy and his kinsmen. The boy's parents and kinsmen make gifts to Brahmins and distribute sweets and money amongst them.

The boy is next taken to his father's house, when a morsel of bread, butter, sugar and *dal* rice *khichri* is given to him. The females also distribute Khichri to the brotherhood, who, in return, give them presents. Till far into the night, songs are sung by the women.

Betrothal, thus effected, creates a kind of relationship so that if one of the parties to it dies, the other is counted impure for three days.

Taking money for a girl is strictly forbidden by the *shastras*, and one who takes it, goes to hell.

Among the Hindus betrothal is a contract and is, as a rule, an indispensable preliminary to the marriage of a girl. If a woman, once married, is remarried on account of divorce or widowhood, the ceremonies performed in the first betrothal are not performed so religiously. Betrothal is of three kinds:

(i) *Dharam* or Pun, in which the girl is given by his parents or guardian, as a quasi-religious offering to her future husband.

(ii) *Waffa Suffa* (Exchange) in which two or more families exchange brides.

(iii) In which a bride price is more or less openly paid.

These kinds exist in modern Hindu system. Briefly these days, the essentials of a valid betrothal are the acceptance of the match, feasting and the exchange of gifts, the religious ceremonies, if observed, are of secondary importance.

The contract of Hindu betrothal is irrevocable, generally, except for certain definite reasons, or in cases when it has become impossible to fulfil. Even when the literal fulfilment is impossible owing to the death of the boy, there is a widespread feeling that an implied contract exists to marry the girl to another member of his family, because a Hindu marriage is more of a relationship between two families, rather than between the boy and the girl alone. The castes and tribes, which allow remarriage of widows, have a strong feeling that the betrothal duly effected gives the boy's family a claim on the girl's hand, so that, in the event of her original fiance's death, she may be married to another boy of the family. The causes, which justify a refusal to carry out a contract of betrothal are mainly physical (e.g., leprosy, impotence, blindness or mental disease in either party), immorality on the part of the girl is generally also a valid reason. The reason of immorality is much more binding on the girl's relatives than on those of the boy. Betrothal is also said to be revocable on other grounds, for example, on the discovery that the parties are within the prohibited degrees of relationship or that they belong to different tribes, and apostasy can also be the reason for revocation.

A promise of marriage (betrothal) cannot be enforced by a suit for specific performance, but a refusal to complete a betrothal or a promise of marriage by an actual marriage would give the injured party a right to recover from the person making the promise, compensation for the loss, if any, sustained by the breach of promise. In case of such breach, a father or guardian, would be entitled to recover money properly spent in contemplation of such marriage. Should the girl die before the marriage, the bridegroom is entitled to recover back the presents given by him to her, subject to paying such expenses as have been incurred.

As a rule, among Hindus, priority of betrothal gives the girl a social, though not legal, claim to be married first, that is to be married before the fiance_ takes another wife. The reason is that in a Hindu household, the first married wife, occupies a more or less privileged position, as against Muslims, where all the four wives are, in the eye of the law at least, absolutely equal.

Pre-Marriage Ceremonies

After betrothal, before a marriage takes place and is given legal effect, certain ceremonies are required to be observed. These ceremonies differ from community to community and from place to place. These ceremonies, sometimes, may look surprising, nevertheless, they are regarded indispensable, as well as highly religious and significant. These are purely social and are meant to increase intimacy between the two families. The boy's father sends sweets etc. for the girl on festivals. These she returns with some money. Later the boy's father sends her ornaments; these too are returned with some cash and clothes, only three or four trinklets are retained.

Pair *Pana* (to put in one's feet) is a ceremony, observed after the betrothal. At this the girl's people send trays of sweets (11-51) to the boy's parents, followed on the same day by a formal visit paid by the women of the boy's family including neighbours and friends, to the girl's house. Refreshment is served, with milk to drink. The mother of the boy blesses the girl; some money circumambulated over the head of the girl is given to the barber maid. When the boy's party has left, the girl's mother and other ladies visit the boy's house. The mother of the girl blesses the boy, gives him a gold coin and a gift to the barber maid. This ceremony is rarely practised in the present times, because the selected couple may be belonging to a distant place.

Milni Ceremony: A few days before the wedding, on an auspicious day; the milni ceremony is performed. Girl's people send trays of sweets to the boy's house. Females do not go with these gifts, only males. They are received by the boy's relatives, assembled for the purpose. The Milni (to meet) is then performed, the girl's party standing on one side and the boy's on the other. The girl's people present money, ornaments to the boy's people and *Salami* (token money) are offered. The counterparts of both sides meet, embrace and offer token money. Nowadays, this ceremony is performed just before the marriage party enters the wedding hall.

Ghodi Ceremony (Riding a Mare): Before the

marriage party (*barat*) proceeds to the girl's house, a mare is sent to the boy's house. The bridegroom rides the mare and a small younger brother/cousin sits behind the bridegroom. The women and relatives in the boy's house, bless the boy and give him and the younger one money. After this ceremony at the boy's house is over. The boy, accompanied by relatives and friends (*baratis*), proceed to the girl's house singing and dancing to the tunes of the band, under the shade of glittering lights.

After the marriage party reaches the bride's house, the boy dismounts the mare and is led to the inner chambers. The Milni is performed and then the rest of the marriage party sits in the auditorium, where some entertainment and light refreshment are served. A practice, that is being performed now is that the boy, before reaching the inner chambers, exchanges garland with the bride.

The Marriage Performance

The marriage party goes to the dining hall. The bridegroom in the inner chamber is surrounded by girls and other females of the bride's house, who jest with him. The girl and her parents observe fast, on this day, till the time after *Saptapadi* (seven steps ceremony). The boy's side (the bridegroom and his parents) also, sometimes observe fast. The mother of the boy never accompanies the marriage party. After Ghodi ceremony, she sees the face of her son only when he comes back with the bride.

When the auspicious moment for the *Lagan* draws near, the boy goes to the *Bedi* (the place decorated with banana tree trunks under the open sky) and the marriage ceremony starts. The boy is seated on a wooden seat and by his side, the girl is also seated. On one side of the couple, the parents of the girl sit, Opposite the father/guardian of the boy sit. On the fourth side, the two priests of either side sit. After yajna with recitation of Vedic mantras, a piece of long cloth hanging on the shoulder of the boy, is tethered to a corner of the *dupatta* (head cover) of the girl. The couple is then made to stand up and they go around the fire seven times (Saptapadi), which include three steps led by the bride and the other steps by the bridegroom. When the seventh round of the consecrated fire has been taken, the marriage becomes complete and binding under the law. Before the seventh step is taken, marriage is incomplete and may be revoked. Thus the performance of Saptapadi is an essential condition of Hindu marriage. During the ceremony and before the seven steps, the priest makes the couple take oaths of responsibilities and duties of a husband and wife. Each round (in all seven) consisted of seven steps, the bridegroom saying to the bride: "Take thou one step for the acquirement of force, take thou two steps for strength, take thou three steps for the increase of wealth; take thou four steps for well being; take thou fifth step for offspring; take thou sixth step for the seasons; take thou seventh step as a friend; be faithfully devoted to me; may we obtain many sons; may they attain to a good old age." Then bringing both their heads into close juxtaposition, someone sprinkles water on them from a jar.

A Hindu bride, on becoming a wife, can be defined in a version of Mahabharata (I. 3028) as:

"A wife is half the man, his trust friend,
A loving wife is a perpetual spring
Of virtue, pleasure, wealth; a faithful wife
Is his best aid in seeking heavenly bliss;
A sweetly speaking wife is a companion
In solitude, a father in advice,
A mother in all seasons of distress,
A rest in passing through life's wilderness."

The wedding rite having been gone through, the Khat *Pujan* is next performed. The bride and the bridegroom are seated on a bed with all presents and gifts given to them.

The boy is asked by the bride's kinswomen to recite a *Chhanda* (couplet), for which he is nominally paid (another zest of the bride's friends).

The couple, led by the bridegroom, to whose long cloth has been tied the headdress corner of the bride, leads out of the house of the bride to the *doli* (carriage). She is seated inside, often with a little girl, to give her company. The bride, on leaving her house, while meeting her father, mother and other kinsmen starts crying, which is continued, even when she gets seated in the carriage. When the departing procession starts, bride's kinsmen go for a certain distance, then they return. The Bridegroom's party with the bride go to their house.

When the couple approach the house, some women of the family receive them with due honour. The mother of the bridegroom receives the couple at the door of the house, pours mustard oil on both sides of the door and allows the couple to enter the house. Immediately after entry, the bride has to topple over small earthen pots full of rice, after which enters the house and is received by the womenfolk. In some places, the mother waves a cup of water seven times round her son and daughter in law, which she then drinks. This means that she, with pleasure and for her son's love, takes on herself every misfortune that may in future time befalls either of them. The senior relatives of the boy in succession put a handful of sesamums into the hands of the girl, which she returns to them at once. This ceremony signifies that they wish the bride to bear children as numerous as the sesamum seeds, which fall on the ground. Then the women sing: "May the bride bear as many sons as sesamum seeds have fallen to the ground."

"Jitne Dharti Til Girese Utne Bahhuti Put Janasi."

The next ceremony is handing over a purse full of money to the bride, and she is at liberty to take as much as she likes. This signifies that the husband entrusts to the care of the wife all his worldly goods. She then promises that she will spend nothing without his knowledge.

One of the after-marriage, very popular ceremony, observed in all Hindu marriages is *Kangana Khelna*. In a large dish, milky water, some colour and *Durba* grass is put. The bride and the bridegroom are made to sit opposite each other, on the sides of the dish. Then both of them are asked to pick out the ring, which is spontaneously thrown in milky water. After a few rounds, the bride opens the knots of the sacred thread tied on the wrist of the bridegroom at the commencement of the wedding ceremonies. This is the last rite of a Hindu marriage.

After a stay of few days, the girl returns to her father's house. The husband visits his father-in-law's house and returns with his wife. This is called *Muqlawa*. The *grehastha* life then continues.

Beautification of the Couple

In every part of the world and in all religions, the bride is decorated—beautified—so as to make her attractive. Some races believe that the decoration should be such as should avoid evil eye. In some tribes, it is believed that the bride should look horrible so that the ghosts get frightened, but mostly she is decorated to look beautiful.

In India, among the Hindus, the bride is beautified with *mehndi* (turmeric paste) applied in artistic designs on her hands and *alta* (red colour) applied on her feet. Black lamp (*kajal*) is applied on her eyes, a red small disc (*bindi*) is fixed on her forehead, ear rings are put in her ears, an ornament (*nathh*) is put on her nose. Anklets adore her feet. Before her decoration, she is rubbed with gram dal paste (*besan*) in oil and then she takes a bath. After bath, she is decorated with ornaments. She puts on gorgeous fast coloured clothes, usually of red colour and sometimes green. In some regions, ivory bangles (*chuda*) is also put on. Around the waist, a girdle of silver or gold is put around, called *kandhoni*. On the fingers of the feet, small designed silver ornaments, called *bichhua* are put on. The decoration is such as to cover all exposed parts of the body of the bride. Since old times, she came out with a long drawn head cloth over the face, but in the modern times, this has changed to just cover the head with the face exposed.

The decoration of the bridegroom is limited to applying mehndi on his hands and putting on a turban, usually of a light red or pink colour. On the previous day, he is also given a massage with Besan in oil. His near relatives, particularly the father, also put on pink coloured turban. In central India, particularly among the tribes, there is a system of tattooing over the body, as is common among African tribes, but among the tribes in northern India, Bihar or the south, this system does not exist. The bridegroom covers his face with a garland called *sehra*. His costume is ordinary and simple. His jewellery is a ring or two on the fingers and a gold necklace. Among the royal families, small jewel earrings are put on.

Marriage Ceremony in Different Regions of India

In Jammu & Kashmir, the bride is decorated with flower ornaments and she puts on sari covered with flowers.

In Maharashtra, seven steps around the fire are not taken, but the bride and the bridegroom stand on two sides of a partitioned place. The priest recites Vedic hymns and with every one step, the bride goes and changes her sari, thus during the ceremony she changes her sari seven times.

On the Malabar Coast, very curious marriage customs exist. The beliefs and practices of some castes in this great tract of India are derived from a book, which is supposed to have been written by an incarnation of God Vishnu. It recites how Parasurama pronounced his commandment to the women (not of Brahmin caste) enjoining them to have promiscuous intercourse with 3-4 Brahmins, before marriage, but this is now forbidden and is no longer in practice.

Girls of the Nair tribe of Malabar go through a curious ceremony called 'tying the *talee*' or marriage string. It is performed before puberty, and the bridegroom is a boy, whose horoscope matches the girl's. The ceremony lasts for four days, going even to the length of a fictitious cohabitation. It terminates with the tearing of a cloth, the pieces of which are given to the boy and the girl, which typifies a divorce. This gives the girl a marriageable status, without which she is said to face excommunication from caste. This ceremony is no longer in practice and has been replaced by the girl's mother making an image of clay adorned with flowers and investing her daughter with the marriage string in the presence of the idol. The Nairs do not adopt the usual ceremony of marriage, but registration of such marriage has been recognized for registration. The Travancore legislative council has passed a law, which recognizes the custom of the presentation of a piece of cloth by a bridegroom to the bride, as a legal form of marriage among Nairs of Travancore.

In Nilgiris, Himalayan regions and among carpenters and blacksmiths of the Malabar coast, polyandrous marriage is celebrated with pomp and show.

In southern India, the practice of infant marriage was recognized among the Brahmins and the higher middle classes of the orthodox Hindus. This practice was copied by lower castes also. A most curious marital method was widespread in the Madras presidency, where an adult girl was married to a mere child and till he grew up, the wife could associate herself with any member of the husband's family or caste. Resulting children, if any, were recognized as the husband's lawful children.

Among the Marvas of Madura, if the betrothed

husband died before marriage, the ceremony of marriage was completed in the presence and on behalf of his corpse, which must be placed on a seat beside the bride. When the rite was over, the Talee (Marriage string) was taken off the bride, and she was free to marry again, whenever she pleased. Similarly in case of adult women, who died before marriage, it was considered unseemly if they arrived in the next world in a state of single blessedness. So, a handsome sum of money was paid to secure a husband for the dead woman and a form of marriage was gone through between her corpse and a living bridegroom. In a caste of Madura, brothers, uncles, nephews and other relations had their wives in common, but outside the family, they were chaste.

All these practices and the ceremonies have been described to give the reader an idea as to what existed before and what has changed by the promulgation of Hindu Marriage Act. These practices do not exist any more, but one would not be surprised if one notices such rites in some remote corners and among some tribal castes.

Among the *banjaras* of Hyderabad (Andhra), the bride had to run away from the marriage pavilion. The priest had to run after her and catch her. The bride's relatives dress the bride with lighter clothes at this time. When the priest is able to catch the bride and tries to make her agree, then the bride's relatives throw rice, beetle nuts and tamarind on the priest. If the priest gets injured and utters a cry, it is considered very auspicious. When the priest comes back with the bride, he is paid an honorarium, and the marriage ceremony is completed.

Among the Urali tribe of Kerala, if a boy has to be married, then the bridegroom's party has to give in return a girl.

Among the tribes of Nicobar Island a system prevails, where a boy enters the room of his fiance at night, and enters her bed. If the girl pushes him out, the matter is over for all times, but if she does not object, then they cohabit together for a month, after which their marriage is performed.

The most remarkable feature of early Hindu family law, in the South was that sonship and marriage seemed to stand in no relation to each other. A man's son need not have been begotten by his father, nor need he have been produced by his father's wife.

In Himachal Pradesh, in the Kulu range, three or four brothers have a wife in common, the eldest is deemed the father of the first born son, the second of the next and so on. Among the monks of Lahul, polyandry arises from the fact that monks, who have no vow of celibacy, enter into monasteries and remain in communion with their elder brother, who stops at home and manages the estate.

In Mahābhārata, princess Draupadi was to marry the one, who achieved a certain extremely difficult feat in archery viz., shooting through the eye of the revolving fish, high-up on a pole. Arjuna alone performed the task and won Draupadi. Under unusual circumstances, Draupadi became a bride for all the five brothers, but she was a supernatural being, who became a virgin after every marriage of all five brothers. These brother Pāndavas were also not ordinary persons, they were the sons of Gods. They were divine. Draupadi's case, criticized sometimes, cannot be judged by ordinary human standards. She had been born with the sole purpose of destroying the Karuavas and she alone could have kept the zeal of the five brothers alive to achieve that.

In Raji tribe of Himachal and Kumaon, as soon as the marriage is settled, half the payment has to be made to the father of the bride immediately.

Among many tribes in Assam, so long as a woman remains unmarried chastity is not usually expected of her and she may dispense her favours, to whom she pleases, but once when she is married, this freedom is no longer tolerated and adultery is very severely punished. In the Arbeg tribe of Assam , marriageable girl tells about her fiance to her maternal uncle, his sons or to her real boy, who is at liberty to run away at getting a chance. He is not attacked, but catching him, he is imprisoned in a room. Thus if he runs away three times and is caught every time, but does not run away the fourth time, then the marriage is settled. On that occasion, all people in the tribe dance and make merry. Invoking the Sun God, the bride and her comrades arrange the feast and the marriage is performed around the fire.

In western region of Tibet, the bridegroom is beaten before marriage. In Ladakh, the system is that when for the first time the bridegroom comes to the bride's house, he is attacked from all sides with kicks, brooms and bamboo. A timid bridegroom runs away, but the true lover tolerates all that and then feasts, merry making and enjoyment are done and he is respectfully treated, the proposed marriage is then accepted.

Among the Korku tribe of Madhya Pradesh, the father of the girl catches hold of a capable boy and brings him home. He is called Lamsena. If the Lamsena likes the girl, he has to fulfil two conditions. Firstly he has to serve as a household servant for 6-12 months, then he has to prove that he has the capacity of a grown man (manhood). To prove his manhood, he has full liberty to have intercourse with the girl, but if the girl does not become pregnant within one year, then Lamsena is made to flee and a new one is caught instead.

There is another tradition among the Korkus, where the girl gets into the house of her fiance. If the boy agrees to marry, the marriage is settled. Otherwise the boy has to leave his house and the village/ tribe and whole of his property becomes that of the girl. A similar tradition is that

Tika ceremony of the Nepalese in Sikkim

the father of the girl sends the daughter away to search for a life companion. Among some Korkus, the father of the girl selects a boy himself. After getting a suitable boy, the terms of payment are settled and the father of the boy takes away the bride.

In Rajasthan and Madhya Pradesh, there is a tribe called Saharia. In the month of *Jeshta* (May), a fair called *Sitabadi* is held. If in the fair, any girl offers a *bidi*, sweets or throws her handkerchief in front of a boy, then it is recognized as a sign of the girl's willingness to marry the boy. This liberty is only allowed for a selection within the tribe Saharia and not outside.

In Madhya Pradesh, a 'Marriage Market' is arranged before the festival of *Holi* (March-April). This is also called *Bhagoria Haat*. Before the Bhagoria, the boy and the girl make out a plan and accordingly the fiance sends an arrow and a bodice to the house of the girl. If the father of the girl accepts the bodice, then with the consent of the two families, marriage is celebrated. If the father does not accept, then the girl is at liberty to go to the Bhagoria market, catch hold of the hand of the boy and run away to a top of the hill.. Then the father of the girl is called there, then he receives the cost from the family of the boy and then accepts the marriage. In Bhagoria market, if a young boy applies red powder (*gulal*) on the face of the girl, then it is considered that the boy wishes to marry that girl.

Among the Bhils of Gujarat, *golgodheri* festival is celebrated on Holi days. On this occasion, *gud* (jaggery) or a coconut is hung on a tree or on the top of a pole, then girls and boys, one over the other, make two circles and dance. The outer circle is that of the boys, and the inner one of the girls. Those who wish to marry have to cross in through the two circles and snatch away the jaggery or the coconut. When such a person tries to pierce through the outer circle, the men in the circle beat him in any way they like. Then next, he tries to pierce through the circle of the girls, then they beat him with sticks. The inner circle is of such women, who are virgins, widows or such as have been married outside the tribe and are willing to have another husband. When the boy succeeds in catching hold of the jaggery or the coconut, then whosoever woman's hand he holds becomes his wife.

Among the Nagas, Gonds and Sabra tribes in India, if a boy offers a garland to a girl and the girl puts on the garland, then it is recognized that she has agreed to marry the man.

In northeast India, if any man offers a garland, in which a bone, feather or skull of an animal has been stitched, it is agreed that such person wishes to marry that girl. If the girl accepts the garland and puts that on, it is a sign that she is agreeable to marry that man. If the girl does not put on the garland and gives that to her brother or father, then it is agreed that the girl recognizes the giver of the garland at par with her brother or father.

Among the Hos of Bihar, the middle man settles the gonang, compensation for the bride, called settlement of *Andi*. The boy's party has to pay the gonang. If on account of the non-payment of the gonang, the marriage is not settled and the girl wishes to marry, then the course open to her is that she goes to the house of the boy with some present . Then the boy's party men can give her any sort of treatment, the Ho society, does not interfere. Sometimes, it also happens that because of a high demand of gonang, the boy's party goes away displeased, but the girl and the boy wish to marry, then the only remedy is for the girl to go to the boy's house with a present. Every effort is then made to make the girl run away. Then, on the initiative of the boy, the girl is called back and the marriage is performed, in front of the tribe's God/ deity.

In Bihar, Madhya Pradesh and among the northeastern tribes, where the system of ghotlu (intercourse before marriage) exists, the girl, before marriage, distributes tobacco among the boys and the girls, but does not give that to her fiance. Then the maid comrades of the girl comb the hair of the boy. The girl distributes combs among all her comrades. Then the couple go away.

Among the Tharuos of Bihar, Madhya Pradesh and northern India, the boy, immediately after the settlement of the marriage, runs away outside the town or at least poses as such. He is run after and is caught. Then *Karai* is settled, which is sent in the form of rice, pulses, etc. to the girl's house, till the marriage is performed. When wine is sent from the girl's house, then preparations for the marriage commence.

Such are the peculiar systems and traditions, still prevailing among the original inhabitants (tribes) of India, irrespective of the passage of the Hindu Marriage Act.

Marriage with Trees, Plants and Inanimate Objects

Among the Hindus, the marriage ceremony is not confined to the nuptial tie between men and women, though rarely it is carried out with regard to trees, plants and many inanimate objects, particularly among the Vaiśnuites. *Tulsi* or holy basil (botanically Ocymum sanctum) is not merely sacred to Viśnu or to his consort Lakśmi, it is pervaded by the essence of these deities, and itself worshipped as a deity as a metamorphosis of Sita, wife of Rama (Viśnu's incarnation). Some this plant with Rukmani, wife of K'rsna, while others hold it to be an embodiment of all the deities together. It is certain, in whatever light regarded, *Tulsi* is the object of more adoration than any other plant at present, worshipped in India. Rosaries of Tulsi beads are worn by Vaiśnuites. According to H.A. Rose, quoting P.N.Q.II P 815, in his book Religious Life of Indian People, "When a wealthy Hindu is without a son, he will marry a Brahmin to a Tulsi plant, which is regarded as a nymph metamorphosed by K'rsna. The ceremonies are solemnized in full and at some expense. The Tulsi is then formally made over to the Brahmin, who is regarded as the donor's son in law for the rest of his life, because he has received his bride at his fictitious father in law's hands."

In western India, an idol of young K'rsna is often brought in procession from the house of one of the Vallabhacharyas, to some rich man's residence, where the Tulsi is kept. The idol is placed in a gorgeous palanquin and followed by a long train of attendants. Then the marriage festivities are celebrated with great pomp and show at the cost of perhaps, several thousand of rupees.

In some other parts of the country, the Tulsi is married to the black *Salagram* pebble (black pebble representing Viśnu or K'rsna, for the God is present in the stone, even without consecration). The pebble bridegroom is placed on the leading elephant/ horse and the marriage party proceeds to the donor of Tulsi plant. It is usual to maintain the supposed matrimonial union between Tulsi and K'rsna, by keeping a leaf of the plant always resting on the Salagram stone.

Trees also play important roles at Hindu weddings and in connection with marriage. There is a social precedence among the trees and Pipal (holy fig trees, botanically Ficus religiosa) is regarded as the Brahmin among all trees. It has a divine personality of its own. It is occupied by the essence of the God Brahma, Viśnu and Śhiva, but specially by Viśnu in his K'rsna manifestation. In the Bhagvad Gita, K'rsna says: "I am *Asvattha* (Pipal) among the trees. It is believed that spirits delight to sit on the branches of these trees and listen to the rustling of the leaves." This tree is sometimes invested with a sacred thread, as if it were a Brahma, all the ceremonies of investiture being performed over it. The mysterious rustling of the tremulous leaves, which resemble those of the poplar, is one cause of the superstitious awe, with which the tree is regarded. No native of India would venture to cut down or in any way injure or interfere with the growth of this tree. Marriage of girls to trees was done with the idea that the dangers of a second marriage should be passed on to the trees. The other idea of such marriage was that the girl would absorb some of its fertility, of the tree. In Orissa, among the Gauras, tree marriage appears in its crudest form, where the girl is taken to the forest and tied to a tree, if not to the mercy of the wild beasts, at least as a prize to the first comer. But usually, it is arranged that some youth of an inferior branch of the tribe, to whom ordinarily she would not be married, carries her away when her people had left her.

Marriage by proxy has also been performed sometimes. The Holkar of Indore sent his sword with a handkerchief tied to it to the bride's house, through a shepherd. The marriage was solemnized with the maharaja. In one instance, a bridegroom, who was very ugly, but in love with a girl and vice versa, sent his Sitar (a string instrument) to the bride's house, which she accepted and came as a bride.

These abnormal type of marriages are performances which occurred in the past, but are no longer in practice. These have been described, with a view to satisfy the curiosity of the reader, who may have heard or read about such marriages from elsewhere.

Hindu Marriage in Modern Age

From the description given above, it is seen that the forms of Hindu marriage, whether recognized by the Dharmashastras or by the consent of the father, cover every mode of matrimonial union between a man and a woman.

In the past, the position of woman deteriorated to such an extent that she had no right worth the name, her keen senses were dulled and without any right or knowledge, she was steeped in ignorance and prejudice. Social prejudices against her were so firmly established that she had hardly any opportunity, freedom or chances of development and self expression. Therefore, reforms were essential. The job was undertaken by Raja Ram Mohun Roy (1772-1833), Ishwar Chandra Vidyasagar (1820-1898), Justice Ranade and others, who started movements to put an end to some of the inhuman practices. As a result, some evil practices were stopped through the passage of certain Acts. All India Women's Conference also contributed to these reforms. Because of the part played by women in the freedom struggle, by picketing liquor shops and foreign goods shops, marching in demonstrations, courting arrests facing lathi charges and bullets, women of the suppressed and degraded, broke all age-old restrictions. Slowly and gradually they acquired more and more rights and came at the level of equality with men. The Hindu Marriage Act, 1955 and The Hindu Succession Act of 1956 removed most of the disabilities from which Indian women were suffering. Rigidity of Śastric rites liberalized and the ceremonies became simpler, although symbolic rites are still in vogue. Now the girl has much to say in the selection of the boy, the marriages last one dinner or so, the Brahmins cut short their period of recitations and all ceremonies have been simplified, but the decorations of the *Pandals*, the lighting, singing and dancing have become very expensive. The pomp and show has increased by far all limits.

However, there is much to be done especially for the womenfolk of the villages, where old prejudices and customs still hold good and are deeply rooted in family life.

Dowry System

Dowry system in Hindu marriages can be called the commercial aspect of the marriage. The practice of giving dowry was very common among all people of all nations. Among Hindus, a girl gets all the domestic utensils, that are necessary to set up a family. Dowry system was prevalent in the Vedic period. In Epic period, gifts from parents, brothers and relatives were recognized as woman's property (*stridhan*). According to Kautilya, "Means of subsistence or jewellery constitutes what is called the property of the woman. It is no guilt for a wife to make use of this property in maintaining her son, her daughter-in-law or herself, if her absent husband has made no provision for her maintenance."

It needs no mention with what evils, the system is fraught. The father of the girl commits suicide, because he has not been able to arrange for the dowry demanded by the parents of the boy. Sometimes the girl herself commits suicide on this account. Due to dowry system, the parents are sometimes compelled to marry the girl to a man, who is almost her father's age. The parents sometimes commit misappropriation or forgery, to arrange for the marriage. Sometimes the girl remains unmarried, because of the dowry demanded by the suitable boy's parents is too high to meet.

Considering the evils of dowry system, The Dowry Prohibition Act 1961 was passed. According to the Act, if a person gives or takes dowry, then he is liable to be punished for an imprisonment and fine. If a person demands directly or indirectly dowry from the guardians of the wife after the marriage has been solemnized, then such a person is liable to be punished for an imprisonment of six months and a fine of Rs 5,000. According to the Act, any contract entered into with a view to taking or giving of dowry is invalid. A dowry, received for the benefit of the wife or her successor, has to be transferred to the wife, otherwise it is punishable under the Act. Under the existing practice, parents supply their daughters with all household furniture, clothes, kitchen utensils, cash, jewels, bedstead and other necessary articles, but these should be without demand or compulsion. All parents do their best for their daughters, but still we find a lot of crimes on account of atrocities on brides, because the demands are made by the husband in collaboration with his parents, particularly the mother, after marriage. Demand for a vehicle or cash money for business or for higher education are some of the reasons put forth. Not being able to meet the demand, some brides are burnt alive or divorced on some other pretext or given the treatment as is worthy of a servant. The dowry, as used to be given, exhibited and shown to all, its giving and taking, has been prohibited by the Act and has been stopped legally, but in reality the evil continues, hidden and secretly. The Act, by itself, is unable to achieve the object, unless public opinion is aroused against the custom.

Conduct of Married Couple

After marriage, the husband has to perform all his necessary duties, and the wife is to be a pattern of perfection. She has to keep all her husband's secrets, never to reveal the amount of his wealth, to excel all other women in attractiveness of appearance, in attention to her husband, in knowledge of cookery, in general cleverness, in ruling her servants wisely, in hospitality, in thrift, in adapting expenditure to income and in superintending every minute circumstance of her family's daily life. She is to cooperate

Decoration in a courtyard (santiya)

with her husband in pursuing the three great objects of life—religious merit, wealth and enjoyment. Neglect of enjoyment is as sinful as to be careless about religion and wealth. Such a perfect wife is called *Padmini*, which means "lotus like". Other kinds are *Chitrini* or a woman of varied accomplishments, *Sankhini* or a conch like woman and the *Hastini* or elephant like.

Definition of a wife has been given in Mahabharata I.3028, which literally translated is as follows:

"A wife is half the man, his truest friend,
A loving wife is a perpetual spring
Of virtue, pleasure, wealth; a faithful wife
Is his best aid in seeking heavenly bliss;
A sweetly speaking wife is a companion
In solitude, a father in advice,
A mother in all seasons of distress,
A rest in passing through life's wilderness."

Smritis, Purānas and Dharamkoshas wrote extensively about wife's duties. The wife must be obedient to the husband. She is to deem her husband to be her God. (Sathāpatha Brāhamana IV. 1.59). The wife shall not discard her husband, even if he were blind, impotent, degenerate, lame or sick (Sancta Likhita Smriti). A good natured wife is to worship her husband, as if he were a God (Manu V.154). The husband is the lord of his wife, he is her God. Only by service to her husband can she retain a higher and noble position (Rāmāyana Ayodhya Kānda 24, 26, 27). Manu Smriti in its fifth chapter, Yagnāvālkya I, 83-87, Viśnu Dharmashāstra 25, 22, Mahābhārata Vanaparva 233.19.58 and Mahābhārata Anuśāsana Parva 123 declare the conduct of virtuous wives. Veda Vyāsa Smriti II. 20,32, Vriddaharita XI.84, Smriti Chandrika Vyrahara Kanda, Madana Parijata and others dwell at length on the duties of a wife.

In Mahābhārata Anuśāsana Parva 126, there is a conversation between Sandili and *Samna* in the talk that took place between Bhishma and Yudhishtra. Sandili was asked how she attained the heavenly abode. Sandili replied to Bhishma thus:

"I reposed confidence in my husband. I did whatever my husband did. I never talked harshly to my husband at any time or on any occasion. I avoided for myself such foods and drinks as are disliked by my husband. I never adorned myself whenever he was away from the village. I served with care and attention, when he returned from his sojourn. I never talked standing on the threshold of my house. I used to get up from my bed early and do my duties. I worshipped the gods, the manes, Brahmins and parents in law. I discharged my family responsibilities. I performed my marital duties."

The Hindu society, as a custom, teaches obedience, performance of duty and spirit of adjustment to women at parental homes.

Adoption

In modern times, children are a luxury to the rich, an encumbrance to the poor. In early ages, female offspring stood in the same position, but male issue was passionately prized. The very existence of a joint family and tribe, surrounded by enemies, would depend upon the continual multiplication of its males. In Hindu families, adoption and inheritance were guided either by *Mitakshara* law or *Dayābhāga* law. These two schools acknowledge the supreme authority of the ancient treatises and commentaries. The Dāyābhaga school prevails in Bengal and the Mitakshara school prevails in other parts of India. These schools differ with regard to the adoption and inheritance of joint family property. The regional location was governed by its specific law. These laws prevalent in different regions, have since been superseded by The Hindu Adoption and Maintenance Act 1956.

Adoption was prevalent in Vedic age. *Aitreye* Brahamana referred to the case of Viswamitra adopting Sunassepha to himself. A *rishi* called Atri was reported to have given away his only son in adoption. As the son of the appointed daughters got property from his mother's father, the progeny of other daughters felt anguished and unhappy. The other daughters could assert their claim to inheritance as time elapsed. With the introduction of the rule that no man should become inclined to marry a brother-less woman, it became rather difficult for such daughters to be married. The son of adopted daughter, however good he might be, was a Sapinda, which is belonging to different gotra. Therefore, the Hindu society had to recognize the need for adoption of a son. The law givers Gautama, Baudhayana and Manu, specified the adopted son's place as that ensuring after *Aurasa* and *Kshetraja* sons. Apastamba made a new approach. Vasishta allotted the adopted son eighth place. Yagnavalkya, Manu and Narada gave the adopted son seventh, sixth and ninth ranks respectively in the order of sons. Whether adoption sprung out of religious motives or secular reasons, was a moot question. This custom received recognition after the fall of Gupta Empire and specifically during the Muslim period. The idea was to keep the property in the family line. Religious outlook was also a reason. The need for a male to perform the obsequies were badly felt. Although the main contributing factor was continuance of family line, yet religious motives prevailed in this regard. Adoption had to be resorted to by a householder in order to escape the tentacles or hell called *Punnama Naraka* (portion of hell set apart for sonless males).

The sonless father would find himself without protection or support in sickness or old age, and would see his land passing into other hands, when he became unable to cultivate it. The necessity for male offspring extended in the case of the Aryan even beyond this world. His happiness in the next world/birth depended upon his having a continuous line of male descendants, whose duty it would be to make the periodical offerings for the repose of the soul. The works in Sanskrit state it to be the first duty of man to become the possessor of male offspring and imprecate the curses upon those, who die without a son. So every contrivance would be exhausted to procure a son, being so indispensable.

The husband was free to adopt a boy, even without the consent of his wife or even in opposition to her views. The widow was enabled to adopt to her husband, either on the authority of her husband or with the assent of the nearest agnates. If the husband died as a member of the joint Hindu family, the widow was bound to obtain the consent of the members of that family. If he died divided, she was to get the assent of the nearest *spindas*.

Her mother-in-law's assent also had some value, but by itself it was not sufficient to warrant adoption. In the case of a prohibition by the husband, the widow was denied the capacity to adopt. The husband had every right to give away their son, even without wife's consent. If the relationship of the natural mother of the adoptee, with the adoptive father, when the woman was unmarried, was not within the prohibited degrees in respect of marriage, then the adoption was valid. This was in force in the presidency of Madras, under the guise of custom, but not in other regions. In the Bombay school, a man could not adopt a daughter's son or sister's son or maternal aunt's son; marriage among these being impermissible. A bachelor or a widow could take a boy in adoption, only a male. Adoption was intended for the welfare and the convenience of the husband. This old system, prevailing in different regions, was superseded by the Hindu Adoption and Maintenance Act of 1956.

According to the Hindu Adaptation and

Maintenance Act 1956, adoption is valid (1) if the person adopting has capacity, and also the right, to take in adoption. (2) If the person giving in adoption has the capacity to do so (3) If the person adopted is capable of being taken in adoption and (4) If the adoption is made in compliance with the other conditions mentioned in the Act. Any male Hindu., who is of sound mind and is not a minor has the capacity to take a son or a daughter in adoption. The consent of the living wife is essential, but if she has renounced the world or has ceased to be a Hindu, or if declared of unsound mind, the consent of the wife was not essential.

Any female Hindu, who is of sound mind, who is not a minor and who is not married, or if married, whose marriage has been dissolved or whose husband is dead or has completely and finally renounced the world or has ceased to be a Hindu or has been declared by a court of Law to be of unsound mind, can take a son or daughter in adoption.

According to the Act, (1) No person except the father or mother or the guardian of a child shall have the capacity to give the child in adoption. (2) The father, if alive, shall alone have the right to give in adoption, but the consent of the mother was essential, unless the mother has completely and finally renounced the world or has ceased to be a Hindu or has been declared by a court of competent jurisdiction to be of unsound mind. (3) The mother may give the child in adoption if the father is dead or has completely and finally renounced the world or has ceased to be a Hindu or has been declared by a court of competent jurisdiction to be of unsound mind. (4) The guardian may give the child in adoption, if both husband and the wife are dead, or have renounced the world, or have ceased to be Hindus or have been declared of unsound mind.

There are other details in the Act regarding persons

who may be adopted, effects of adoption, right of adoptive parents, cancellation of valid adoption prohibition and so on. This Act, now, is in force, in all regions of India.

Divorce

The last aspect of the custom of Hindu marriage is divorce. Divorce is unknown to the general Hindu Law, but is allowed by certain tribes in certain localities, where it is allowed by custom. A divorce by mutual agreement is recognized by law. In general, divorce is something alien to Hindu view point. Hindus consider marriage as a sacrament that is regarded unbreakable throughout life. Even if the husband and the wife have different and opposite views, yet they are bound to live together. There is no reference of divorce in the whole of Vedic literature. According to Manu Smriti, religion of Dharma is based on the lifelong mutual respect for each other by the wife and the husband. In Dharmashāstras, there are some references of leaving each other, the husband or the wife; but these are not synonyms of divorce. Even when such was the case, the wife was entitled to her maintenance and livelihood. According to Kautilya in Arthashāstra, if there is mutual enjoy or jealousy between the wife and the husband, they can leave each other, but consent of both is necessary. These were in accordance with contemporary circumstances and conditions. Present age believes in providing equal opportunities to each.

Basic functions of the family are (1) The regulations of sexual behaviour and reproduction. Manu, the ancient law giver, regarded sexual satisfaction as the aim of family. Vatsayan also looked upon sexual satisfaction as the primary objective of the family. (2) Production and rearing of children. The task of race perpetuation has always been an important function of the family. The Hindu scriptures hold that the religious activities of men cannot be consummated unless he has a son. In the Hindu marriage, the bridegroom says to his bride that I accept you in order to obtain good progeny. (3) Cooperation and division of labour (4) Primary group satisfaction, religious in nature. Family is the centre of religious training for the children, who learn from their parents various religious virtues. In the old family system, different religious practices like image worship, yajna, religious discourses and sermons by pundits were carried on, which made the outlook of the children religious. (5) Educational. The family is an important educational agency. The child learns the first letters under the guidance of the parents, though today, he learns in a kindergarten school. (6) Health. Similarly, the functions relating to health which were performed in the old family, have now been transferred to hospitals and nursing homes. (7) Recreation. The old family provided recreation to its members; singing, dancing and visiting family relations or historical places together. The clubs and hotels have now replaced this old custom. (8) Civic. Family is the school of civil virtues. The child learns the first lessons of citizenship in the family. The virtues of love, cooperation, tolerance, sacrifice, obedience and discipline, which make the child grow into a good citizen. The family has thus been called 'The cradle of civil virtues'. (9) Social customs, mores and folkways. Knowledge was imparted by the family, which exercises social control, as the custodian of culture and serves as 'the natural and convenient channel of social continuity'.

Thus, on account of its strategic position, the family exerts a persistent, intimate and far reaching influence on the habits, attitudes and social experiences of the child as the married couple. Since the old joint system of patriarchal family is on the decline, guide posts for a successful marriage can be enumerated as follows:

(i) Building of a union that is just to both the husband and the wife. (ii) Decision must be made on the basis of what is good for both, not the selfish or narrow wish of either. (iii) No demand should be made by either, that requires a drastic change in the personality. (iv) Too great concentration should be avoided (v) There should be no holding on to the present, nor seeking to bring back the past. Each moment is good and new in itself. (vi) Sensitiveness should not be cultivated. Feelings of either should not be hurt. Complete trust in each other is essential. (vii) Marriage is a lifelong programme of growing together. (vii) There should be natural affection, instead of blind love and (ix) Marriage is not merely sex adjustment. It is life adjustment, of which sex is a part.

There should be mental adjustment between the partners. If mental discord and frustration are to be avoided, there must be greater general understanding of the realities of sex life and divorce should not be viewed as an automatic solution for every disharmony in the family. Elimination of needless annoyances, holding frank discussions, but avoiding arguments over problems, being just and not expecting always justice, working out plans together; giving special attention to larger areas of agreements, avoiding quarrels over non essentials and overlooking petty differences and playing the role of a sportsman, are some of the measures to reduce marital conflicts.

The Modern Family

In the early historical period, patriarchal (father dominated) joint family system existed. A new age of science and democracy ushered in after the Renaissance and Reformation, which undermined the foundations of patriarchal joint family system. Economic factors, industrialization, urbanization and mobility broke down the self sufficiency of the joint family system. Many cultural factors, the growth of democratic ideals and the decline of religious orthodoxy resulted in 'person centered democratic' type of a family. The growth of urbanization, women and daughters becoming as good the earning members of the family as the men and sons, gainful employment of women, substitution of home made commodities by ready-made commodities, use of appliances in cooking, baking, washing and rearing up of children saved much energy and time of the housewife and social mobility has cut still deeper into the family organization. The crucial factors like the democratic state curbed the domination of the patriarch over the family members. The right to vote became an individual right. The religious functions of the family diminished. The view that the family was a divine creation and the patriarch was the symbol of God became less accepted. Ernest R. Mowrer wrote: "The husband is no longer the head of the household in many families, in spite of the fact that he still provides the family name. In fact, he is lucky if his children look upon him other than as a meddlesome outsider." Marriage is no longer a devotion of woman to man but contracting to live together on equal terms. It has wrought deathknell to a patriarchal family and brought in modern family, which is very much different in structure and function from the traditional family.

In modern family, there is decreased control of the marriage sacrament. Male dominance and female obedience have decreased. The people are less subject to parental control concerning marriage, whom and when they shall marry. Marriage is now settled by the partners themselves, choice of the mate by the mate, usually the result of courtship or falling in love, although rural areas are yet free from such modernization. The woman in the modern family is an equal member with equal rights, under no subjugation, so the husband has to request the wife to do a task. The woman can now divorce her husband as the husband can divorce her. She can sue the husband for her rights and likewise be sued. The rigidity in sexual relationship, traditionally associated, no longer characterizes the modern family. Economic independence has been attained by women in the modern family.

MacIver and Page write, "Not only the economic and the religious changes, but the whole process of modern civilization has worked towards giving woman a new position in society, the family and specially in relation to man, her husband."

The liberal use of the contraceptives and their generous supply has cultivated the idea of a small family, as against the joint family. The modern family is secular in attitude. The religious rites of the traditional family viz., early prayer, yajna, etc. are no longer performed in a modern family. Marriage has also become a civil contract rather than a religious sacrament. It can be dissolved at any moment. The authority of religion over the conditions of marriage and divorce has markedly declined. Divorce is on the increase, as against the traditional family, where it was a rare phenomenon. Birth of the child at home, teaching at home, cooking, washing and such household jobs have now been taken over by specialized agencies such as nursing homes, kindergarten school, hotels and laundries. Prepared and manufactured goods are more and more consumed in modern families, as against the traditional family. The modern family is a trend towards filocentric family, where the children tend to dominate the scene and their wishes determine the policy of the family. The children now decide which school they want to go, what clothes they want to wear and what food should be cooked for them. The choice of the movie is also as per selection by the children. Thus the patriarchal joint family, the traditionally established system, has been subjected to profound modifications of an economic, social and biological nature. Ceremony and religion have lost almost all connection with the home as an entity.

The traditional family was a stable type of family, whose dissolution was rarely thought of and was not very easy. It faced the world as a unit. Women outside the family had no refuge. Social mobility was slight, but it has all changed. There is lack of mutual trust. The marriage bonds have weakened. A long process of mutual alienation between the husband and the wife results in a divorce, for which the law has made provisions in (The Hindu

Marriage Act of 1955, as amended and modified in 1960, 1964, 1976 and 1978). The Act provides that any marriage shall be avoidable and may be annulled by a decree of nullity on any of the following grounds:

(i) That the marriage has not been consummated owing to the impotence of the respondent;

(ii) (a) That the respondent, at the time of the marriage is incapable of giving a valid consent to the marriage in consequence of unsoundness of mind;

(b) Though capable of giving a valid consent, has been suffering from mental disorder of such a kind or to such an extent as to be unfit for marriage and the procreation of children or

(c) has been subject to recurrent attacks of insanity or epilepsy;

(iii) That the consent of the petitioner or where the consent of the guardian in marriage of the petitioner was obtained by force or by fraud as to the nature of ceremony or by or to any material fact of circumstance concerning respondent (petition has to be filed within one year after the force has ceased to operate or as the case may be the fraud has been discovered); and

(iv) That the respondent was at the time of marriage pregnant by some person other than the petitioner (if the petitioner was ignorant of that fact and if the petition is filed within one year from the date of marriage and marital intercourse with the consent of the petitioner has not taken place).

Either of the parties to the marriage may pray for Divorce on the following grounds:

(i) That the other party has after the marriage voluntary sexual intercourse with any person other than the spouse;

(ii) That the respondent has treated the petitioner with cruelty;

(iii) That the respondent has deserted the petitioner for a continuous period of not less than two years immediately preceding the presentation of the petition (desertion without reasonable cause and without the consent or against the wish of the petitioner);

(iv) Has ceased to be a Hindu by conversion to another religion;

(v) That the respondent has been incurable of unsound mind, or has been suffering continuously or intermittently from mental disorder of such a kind and to such an extent the petitioner cannot reasonably be expected to live with the respondent;

(vi) Has been suffering from a virulent and incurable form of leprosy;

(vii) Has been suffering from venereal disease in a communicable form;

(viii) Has renounced the world by entering any religious order;

(ix) Has not been heard of as being alive for a period of seven years or more;

(x) Not living together for a period of one year or more after an order for judicial separation;

(xi) That the order for restitution of conjugal rights was not obeyed.

The wife, alone can file a petition for divorce on the following grounds:-

(i) That the respondent marrying a woman before the commencement of the Act or that any other wife of the husband marrying before such commencement was alive at the solemnization of the marriage of the petitioner;

(ii) That the husband has been guilty of rape, sodomy or beastility; or

(iii) The parties, not living together after maintenance was ordered to be given to the wife;

(iv) In the case of petitioner's marriage before attained the age of 15 years, if she repudiates the marriage after attaining the age of 18 years (whether the marriage has been consummated or not);

The parties to the marriage can get a divorce by mutual consent on the following grounds:

(i) That the parties have been living separately for a period of one year or more and

(ii) That they are not able to live together, and that they mutually agree to the dissolution of the marriage.

Usually the petition for divorce under the above clause must be filed only after one year from the date of marriage. Progeny, which was of great importance and significance, before the Act in traditional system, is of little importance now. At present no man can discard his wife on the ground that she could not beget children for him. Traditional system of marriage as a sacrament, family relations, joint family system, rights of women, provisions for divorce, has all undergone a change in the Hindu system of living, by enactment of the Acts, briefly described herein.

India being an agricultural country, where most of the population lives in the villages, there is not much change in the rural families, where joint family system, agricultural economy, interdependence of members and homogenous relationships, domination of the family, strong discipline, authority of the family head and mutual cooperation and impersonal relationship amongst members of the family, traditional customs and ceremonies, still are in practice.

In spite of all the enactment, liberalization of laws and modernization, the Hindu family has largely maintained customs of dowry and adoption, though in a much simplified manner. Divorce, though legalized, is least among Hindu couples.

A Hindu housewife is still an ideal woman like Sita of the Ramayana or Rukmini of the Mahabharata.

CHAPTER IV
Death And Funeral Rites

BEFORE WE describe the death and funeral rites among the Hindus, one must learn about an established fact that the Hindus believe in transmigration of soul and the doctrine of *Karma*. So, whatever one does, good or bad, one has to reap its fruits, if not in this life, in lives to come. All actions of man result in Karma, from which there is no escape. Transmigration is the movement of soul at death from one life to next. In Hinduism the view, that human existence is an unending series of earthly lives with the soul transmigrating from one to the next, has always been linked with the idea of Karma and the religious quest has been an effort to find a way of escape from this continuing existence.

Karma is basically 'action', hence the results of action, the belief that one's own deeds in this and the past life determine the circumstances of one's present life of happiness or sufferings, of caste and sex. Thus Karma is the belief that whatever one's present conditions are, one has earned it by his own past deeds.

In the *Dharmashāstras*, the Hindu Law books on duty and virtue, the belief in Karma and transmigration is taken for granted and has become part of the basic form of reference.

The Hindu doctrine in regard to the spirits of the dead, states two conditions into which they are supposed to pass. They may be degraded to the state of evil demons or elevated to the position of divinities. In the former case, they are feared and propitiated than worshipped; in the latter case they are revered and worshipped. Homage to dead relations in all forms of religious devotion is paid. It is an element in the creed of nearly every race. The Roman catholic church teaches that supplications and prayers may avail to improve the condition of departed spirits in purgatory. Special masses offered to the souls of deceased relations and prayers for the dead have been introduced into regular mass. In some Roman catholic countries 'All Saints Day' is observed, where great feasting takes place and the souls of the dead are supposed to join in the festivities and consume the essence of the food before it is eaten. According to the Bishop of Petersborough, in early church while awaiting their final consummation and bliss, the souls of the faithful, being free from all suffering, were capable of a progress in holiness and happiness. And that prayers for such progress might lawfully be made on their behalf. Accordingly prayers for 'the rest and refreshment of the departed' abound in the early liturgies of the church. In German and Switzerland church called Schadel-haus (Skull house). It was customary to exhume skeletons at intervals of several years and place their skulls in a small chapel adjoining the Parish church, which is used as an oratory, where people pray for their dead relations and friends. Periodical advertisement in loving memory of the dead is another custom published in the obituary of the newspapers.

The Evil and Demon Spirits

The evils of all kinds—difficulties, dangers and disasters, famines, diseases, pestilence and death are thought by an ordinary Hindu to proceed from demons and devils. In earliest Hindu religious thought demoniac influence was always an essential ingredient supposed to have originated as the peopling of the air by spiritual beings — the personifications or companions of storm and tempest. In

India, a great number of the people worship 'Fear'.

Indian Sanskrit Literature makes constant mention of numerous regions above and below the earth which serve as abode of such beings. The Epics and the *Purānas* mention seven upper and seven lower worlds with 21/28 hells beneath the latter.

The seven worlds including the world we live in are inhabited by countless hosts of superhuman and semi divine creatures of all kinds. For those, who have attained a state of absolute perfection, some of the highest worlds have apparently been set apart for occupation by those beautiful creatures. Such categories are the *Siddhas* and others.

The region just above the earth, corresponding to the atmosphere called *Bhuvar*, is the abode of numerous demonized spirits of dead men, superhuman beings, who like the men of the lower world may be termed Demons. They may be pious or impious, benevolent or malevolent, merciful or cruel, but are generally gifted with free will and may have good or evil characteristics. They may be obedient to Gods as *Ganas* (servants) or may be opposed to them as *Asuras*. Similarly they may be friends or enemies of men. Some of them are constantly traversing the earth and the world immediately above the earth. They are innumerable, as many as 330 million Gods. Their number is constantly replenished, with new inhabitants from the world of human beings. They are wholly spiritual and immaterial. They have finer frames and ethereal structures, and not necessarily visible to man. Yet their frames have essential elements gross material particles. Their corporeal organization stands midway between that of men and Gods, just as the Gods have forms (incarnations).

Gods, demons and men are so closely connected and interrelated that it is difficult to draw any line of demarcation between them. All three have bodies made up of gross elementary particles, ethereal in case of Gods, less ethereal of demons and earthly in case of men. All three have sex distinctions. All men living on the earth can be categorized as those who have divine nature (*Daiva*) and those who are demoniac (*Asura*). There are instances of demons allaying themselves with mortal women.

The gross body is of three kinds—divine, earthly and intermediate. Intermediate body is one of the departed spirit, a subtle frame, invested after the burning of the earthly gross body and during the interval preceding the assumption of another earthly gross body.

This intermediate body is called *Preta*. This serves as a cover for the departed soul till its residence in the world of spirits called *Pitrilok*. This body, as already explained, is of a more ethereal substance than earthly bodies. All spirits, according to the Hindu transmigration doctrine, have to pass through this intermediate temporary paradise before assuming new terrestrial body.

The demons (demoniac spirits) may possess extra number of hands and arms, just like the secondary deities. The demons have the power of assuming any shape they like and moving through the air in all directions like the Gods. In the Epics the bodies of Gods have been described as very similar to those of men. They differ only in the power of walking above the surface of the earth in being shadowless, being free from perspiration, having eyes that never wink and flowery ornaments that never wither (Nala Damayanti episode in the Mahabharata). The demons are generally dwarfish and shorter than men, but they enjoy the faculty of assuming any shape suited to their needs and can even assume the shape of men.

There are two great divisions of such spirits; one created by the Gods at the creation of the world and brought into the world as demons (*Gunas*), who act at the orders of the superior deities as Nandi of Lord Śiva or the demons, who were ordered by Śiva to destroy the *yajna* by Daksheye

Prajapati. The second division comprises of those demons, whose creation is due to man -to the spirits of men, who have once lived upon the earth. The existence of these demons is derived from departed spirits of dead human beings and it is to these that adoration and propitiation are commonly offered. All malignant devils are believed to have been originally human beings. If a man is killed by a tiger or dies as a result of snake bite and does not receive proper funeral ceremonies, he is believed to become an unquiet spirit, roaming about with malevolent proclivities. Death in an accident and formal disposal without proper funeral ceremonies or deaths inflicted by criminals and disposal of the body secretly without proper rites turns the intermediate body into ghosts — roaming spirits.

In Southern India, it is a firm belief that if a notorious man dies his evil nature never dies and his every vice assumes personality and lives after him as a demon. This equally applies to women, so the demons may be of either sex, of any caste and thus demons may be of all ranks and may have either refined or low tastes, as deceit devils, lying devils, gambling devils and so on. A criminal who dies, his sins and crimes live after him in the shape of malignant demons, as murder devils, theft devils, adultery devils and so on. Such demons are always on the lookout for weak minded people instigating them to commit crimes of similar nature. Personified diseases, calamities, disasters, hailstorms are believed to be demons.

These lower forms of evil demons, once the occupants of human bodies, are most dreaded by the generality of Hindus and therefore most worshipped. These are of three classes—*bhuta*, preta and *pisācha*.

Bhuta is spirit emanating from a man, who has died a violent death either by accident, suicide or capital punishment, and has not had proper funeral ceremony performed afterwards.

A Preta is the spirit of a deformed or crippled person or of one defective in some limb or organ or of a child that dies prematurely owing to the omission of ceremonies during the formation of the embryo. It may not necessarily be an evil disposed spirit.

A Pisācha is a demon created by a man's vices. It is the ghost of a liar, drunkard, adulterer or a criminal of any kind or of one who died as insane. The *Pisāchas* are malicious and mischievous imps and friends. They haunt cemeteries or take up their abode in trees. They may take hideous or beautiful shapes and even the form of men. Animal blood is their pet food but generally believed to feed on corpses and may even occupy and vivify dead bodies. They may even enter human beings through the mouth and may cause diseases and unpleasant affections of all kinds. They may take the shape of a dog, cat, serpent or other animal.

There is no real worship to these demons. There are no temples raised to them. The only place of worship is a mere heap of earth piled up in a pyramidal shape, near some tree, or a similar erection formed with bricks and painted with streaks of white. No real prayers are said at such shrines, but offerings of food may be made.

In southern India devil worship is more systematically practised as compared to the North. *Demonophobia* is prevalent all over the south. The reason for this could be the prevalence of *Śaivism* on a wide scale or that during southern invasion the Dravidian met with the aboriginal tribes, whose whole aspect and demeanor appeared to them to resemble those of demons. As the Aryans advanced their excited imagination converted these powerful enemies into supernatural giants and the most formidable of them into veritable demons (*Rakshas*). In due course, Aryans, Dravidians and aboriginal blended amicably together but the dread of demons remained and is still prevailing. The lower castes-the Shanars are so scared of the South, that they never face the doors of their houses towards the South, lest the Evil spirits should enter their houses from that direction.

The more, we go to the south, nearer Sri Lanka, we find the people steeped in demonolatry and saturated with every form of superstitious fear of evil spirits, ghosts and mischievous ugly demons. Therefore devil worship and propitiation persist among the villagers, who make a life size baked clay horse in their fields, in honour of male guardian god Ayenar, who is believed to be a daring horseman and the most active anti-demonist. Offerings and other oblations are presented to these clay horse god images.

The Shanars, whose occupation is cultivating and climbing the Palmyra tree for the sake of the juice, consider every malady to be the more superstitious, inflicted by a devil and that a sacrifice is necessary for its removal. Unusual severity or continuance of any disease are proofs of possession by the devil spirit. According to Bishop Caldwell, when a woman is heard to weep and laugh alternately, without any adequate cause, or shrieks and looks wild, when no snake or wild beast can be perceived, the devil is supposed to be the cause of the mischief. The Shanara doctor is called in, but when he finds no description of the hysterical complaints, he pronounces that the devil has taken possession of the woman and that a sacrifice be offered with a cloth and a white fowl to the doctor. To expel the devil, moving ceremonies and powerful incantations, tried during the course of times, are performed. If the devil should prove an obstinate one and refuse to leave, his retreat may generally be hastened by the vigorous application of a slipper or a broom to the shoulders of the possessed person, the operator uses most scurrilous language all the time. After a time, the demon loses his downcast, sullen look, gets angry and writhes about under the slippering and at length cries, "I go, I go". Then they ask him his name and why he came there. He tells them that he is such and such devil, whom they have neglected and that he wants an offering. Or he calls himself by the name of some deceased relative, who has become a demon, previously unimagined by the relatives. On the demon agreeing to leave, the beating is stopped and immediate arrangements are made for a sacrifice to appease the evil spirit. The possessed person awakes from a sleep and appears to have no knowledge of anything that has happened.

In Kanara, the most feared demons are Kalkatti, Kallurti and Panjurli. Kalkatti and Kallurti were the son and daughter of Kalkuda, a sculptor. Kalkatti made the celebrated Jain statue at Karakal, and later still better one at Yenur. The king of Karakal cut off the left hand and right leg of Kalkatti, so that he should not make a better statue, as made by him at Karakal, but still he made one at Yenur. Kalkatti and his sister Kallurti lived at Yenur and in order to take revenge on the king of Karakal, burnt his palace and the town, thus annoying people. These two are considered formidable demons. Panjurli is a terrible pigfaced demon, created by the curse of Śiva.

In South Kanara, according to Walhouse, there is a noted temple, said to be the abode of seven most dreaded demons. Devil stones inherited by Bhuta are sold there, which are purchased and used by the people to ward off enemies.

There are other methods of neutralizing the evil influences of demons prevalent in Southern India, described by Monier Williams. Male and female devils are supposed to delight in dancing, particularly when accompanied with wild cries, violent gesticulations, ringing of bells and noisy discordant music. Hence, when pestilence is rife in a district, professional exercises, or certain persons elected for the purpose paint their faces, put on hideous masks, dress up in fantastic garments, arm themselves with strange weapons and commence dancing. Their object is to personate particular devils or rather perhaps to induce such devils to leave the persons of their victims and to occupy the persons of the dancers, who shriek, fling themselves about and work themselves up into a frenzy of excitement, amid beating of tom-toms, blowing of horns and ringing of bells. When the dancers are thoroughly exhausted by their gesticulations, they sink down in a kind of trance and are then believed to be actually possessed by the spirit of the demon and are turned for a time into demon-mediums, gifted with clairvoyance and a power of delivering prophetic utterances. The spectators ask them questions about missing relatives or future events and their deliverance is supposed to be oracular.

At Tanjore, one of the most popular festivals called Illecchi Da Nema, for neutralizing the evil influence is celebrated every fifteen or twenty years. In another festival, called Kallyata, a wild dance is performed every sixtieth year in front of a particular rock or stone, which is supposed to tremble and shake periodically. Sometimes the performance takes place in a large shed in the middle of which burns a common lamp under a canopy, around are images of the *Bhutas*.

At the distance of about a foot in front of the lamp, a common wooden tripod stand is placed, on which is constructed a square frame of coconut leaves. Inside this frame, a quantity of rice and turmeric is piled up into a pyramid, into which a three branched iron lamp is inserted. The offerings are arranged around. The offerings consist of fruits and living victims, such as fowls and goats. The latter are adorned with garlands and both are then decapitated, the warm blood being either poured out on the ground or on the altar or else drunk by the officiating priest. The idea is that the demon thirsts for blood and becomes irritated if his cravings are not satisfied. The whole object of sacrificing animal is to assuage his thirst and appease his anger. After these preliminaries, the principal performance takes place in an open space in front of the slaughtered victims. The priest or some other devotee, who has undergone a long preparatory fasting, comes forward to personate a particular demon. He is dressed up in a fantastic costume, often covered with grotesque dangling ornaments and jingling bells. Sometimes he wears a hideous mask; sometimes his face is dabbed with paint of different colours. In one hand he holds a sword, trident or other implement and perhaps a bell in the other. He then commences dancing or pacing up and down in an exciting manner, amid beating of tom-toms, blowing or horns and all kinds of noisy music, while an attendant sings songs or recites rude poems descriptive of the deeds of the demons. Meanwhile spirituous liquor is distributed, the performer becomes violently excited and the demon takes complete possession of him. Finally he succumbs in a hysterical fit and gives out oracular responses to any inquiry addressed to him. Most of the bystanders consult him as to their several wants and destinies or the welfare of absent relatives, but are not allowed to do so without presenting offerings first.

On the western coast, the custom of appeasing the demon (Bhuta) is different. There, in the villages, in every house, a cot is kept on the ground or suspended by ropes, as the abode of the Bhuta. The object is the propitiation of the spirit of the devil. On the last day of every lunar month, flowers are placed on the cot and incense is burnt before it. Once a year, in the month of April, a ceremony called Tambila is performed. During this ceremony, fried rice mixed with coarse sugar is made into a ball and is placed on plantain leaves and put on the cot. A lighted torch is placed in front of the ball, duly turned yellow with turmeric. A fowl with its throat cut, is held above the ball and light and the blood is allowed to drop on the ball. If any member of the family be stricken with some unusual attack, then the face of the fowl is turned towards him and the neck of the fowl is twisted and the blood is allowed to fall on him. The priest is consulted to recommend alms to be given to him, to satisfy hostile stars, with a promise to perform special ceremony to the Bhuta. The aim of the ceremony is to offer life for life.

An annual festival called *Kolla* is held at *Bhutasthan*, the shrine of the Bhutas, where brass images roughly made in human figures or resembling pigs, tigers, fowls, etc. are kept. The festival always takes place at night. All the villagers assemble. The *pujari* takes the Bhuta sword and a bell in his hands and whips round and round, imitating the supposed gestures of the demon. A *Dheda* (*Dher*), a man of low caste comes forward naked, except round the loins; head, face and body besmeared with white, yellow and red paint. Against the beat of the drum, he breaks into a maniac dance, capering, bounding and spinning vehemently. At last he stops and speaks like a demon, in loud hoarse commanding tones. Cases of disputes, litigation is then brought before him and the *Dhera* pronounces awards. Then the Dhera eats food and animal food (if of low caste) and drinks juice.

Some sorcerers, if called upon to get rid of an enemy mould a human effigy in wax, pronouncing over it a few mysterious cabalistic words. The waxen figure is then placed before a fire and as it melts brings down deadly calamities on the head of the person to be destroyed. Or, if a human bone from the cemetery can be procured and certain Mantras recited over it, very fatal results will ensue. Whatever the claim may be, the fact is that no magician, wizard, sorcerer or witch, whose feats are recorded in history, biography or fable, has ever pretended to be able to accomplish by incantations and enchantment, half of what the Mantra *Shāstris* claim to have power to effect by help of the Mantras.

In some parts of India, a tiger's claw or tooth is worn on the neck and is held to be very efficacious against the misfortunes which may at any time be brought about by the malicious spirits or by evil influences.

In some places, an image of *Linga* is worn, or some bright ornament such as a string of white cowries (small shells of snails found on sea coast), which is supposed to arrest evil glances or divert them from the person wearing such a necklace. A small iron ring is also commonly carried about as an amulet. It is perfectly effective if it is inlaid with pearls.

Frequently a lime is carried in the turban with a great faith in its prophylactic properties.

Any ornament with a figure of Hanuman engraved on it makes an admirable charm, which few demons can withstand. To ward off evil eye, a common custom is to put up a small earthen pot in front of the new house under construction, on which eyes, nose are drawn in black on its face.

Patāla: Lower Regions

All seven upper worlds and seven lower worlds are believed to rest on the thousand heads of the great serpent Sesha; or the earth, which is the lowest of the seven upper worlds, is supposed to be supported at the quarters and intermediate quarters of the sky by eight male and eight female mythical elephants. Then again the earth is thought to be composed of seven great circular islands (*Jambu, Kusa, Plaksha, Salmali* and such other names of trees), surrounded by seven seas, described in the Mahābhārata VI.236, etc. and *Viśnu Purāna* II.2, etc.

The seven worlds, immediately below the earth, are not places of punishment at all. According to Viśnu Purāna II.5, they are the regions adorned with beautiful palaces, groves and streams, where the sun diffuses light but not heat and the moon shines for illumination, not for cold, where the air resounds with the song of birds, where all delicious foods, beverages are at hand for those who wish to enjoy.

All the seven lower regions and especially the one Patāla, are inhabited by demoniac creatures viz.: *Daityas* and *Dānavas*. Daityas are the supposed children of the Goddess Diti, wife of Kashyap; as opposed to the Gods, who are the children of Aditi, another wife of Kashyap. Dānavas are the daughters of Danu. These two classes occupy some of the lower seven regions, of which Patāla is one, which appears to belong to a higher order of creation than the *Rākshasas*. The nature of Rakshasas is inclined to baser forms of wickedness and whose malignity is more particularly directed against men.

Daityas and Danavas are not necessarily wicked and are in some respects superior to men and notably by a race of half men and half serpents, called *Nāgas*. These serpent demons, said to have jewels on their heads, have sprung up from Kadru, wife of Kashyap and some of the females, Nāga *Kanyās*, are even said to have married human heroes as has been filmed in some Hindi pictures. Three chief serpents Sesha, Vasuki and Takshaka, rule over these serpent demons and also over other ordinary snakes, which infest the earth.

The Hell (*Naraka*)

Below the seven lower worlds, are twenty-one hells. Viśnu Purāna and the *Bhagvata*, make it twenty eight in number. The hells are for infliction of punishment and suffering on sinful persons. They are merely temporary purgatories intended for the purpose of purifying those who have led wicked lives. The description of hells differs one from the other; one may be complete darkness, the other a dense forest, another with heated caldrons (*Tapata Kumbha*) comparable to Roman Catholic fourth dungeon with boiling kettles. In some other hells there may be red hot charcoal or blood, the leaves of trees resembling sharp swords; another a sea of fetid mud and yet another a plain paved with iron spikes.

Haunted Houses

Before concluding the topic 'Spirits of the Dead', sometimes a reference is made to haunted houses, as the dwelling place of the spirits of the dead. In this connection, a vivid description has been given in June 9, 1883 number of 'Graphic', which is reproduced here:

"The notion of Indian houses being haunted is, on first thought rather ridiculous. Nevertheless, there is scarcely a station in Hindustan which has not its haunted bungalows. The spirits appear to have appalled beholders by sunlight as well as by night, and are apparently indifferent to the time of the day. A curious and very well authenticated instance of this disregard of the Hour is that of an afternoon ghost, which punctually appears at sunset in a certain house at Madras (Chinnai).

"But there are evil and beneficent spirits in India. There is a well known haunted house in one of the stations in North of India, where the 'House ghost', if we may so call him, evinces malicious and malignant idiosyncrasies. It is the wretched spirit's mundane amusement to try and upset the *charpoy* or bed, on which the bewildered tenant seeks repose; and so persistent are his efforts in this direction that they have been compared to shocks of earthquake, and to the explosions of subterranean mines. People laugh, but no one particularly cares to sleep twice in that haunted bungalow.

"Another species of malignant spirit, which becomes more intimately associated with an Indian house is Disease. There are houses in Indian towns and stations, of which the citizens say it as much as any man's life is worth to enter them. A particular person, superior to superstition and considering it 'such rot', went into such a house and speedily lost his wife and three children. It cannot be denied that the mortality in some Indian bungalows of an unlucky reputation, is unaccountable. These ghosts have done the living no end of good. The warnings and other information, they have imparted, have been endless."

Having discussed as to what happens to the soul (spirit) of the dead among Hindus, we now pass on to the observance and performance of rites, before death and the funeral rites.

Rites before Death

When a person is in extremes, nearing death, he is made to give away some grain, money and a cow in charity. A Pundit is sent for to recite verses from the *Bishan Sahasrnam* and *Bhagwat Gita*. This pundit is different than the one, who performs *puja* (worship) ceremonies. The one who functions at death ceremonies is called a Panda. Many such Pandas are seen at such places as Hardwar, Prayag (Allahabad) and banks of river Narmada, where people go to dispose off bones, etc. of the dead after cremation. The orthodox alms are: (i) *Gaudan* or a gift of a cow, whose horns are ornamented with gold or silver rings, while her neck is garlanded with flowers and her body covered with a piece of new cloth — usually red. Copper coins are placed at her feet, and she is led up to the dying person, who gives her to the Panda (*Vedwa* Brahmin), who prays that she may lead the dying man by the tail to the next world. The donor also pours a few drops of water into the Panda's hands. (ii) *Raskka*'s Gifts of sugar, alkali, soap, cotton and other necessities of life are given to the Panda. (iii) *Dipa*, an earthen lamp, containing a silver or gold coin is placed in the palm of the dying person, and after the recital of mantras, is given to the Panda. The tail of the cow is given in the hand of the dying person, with the belief that the tail of the cow, will enable the dying person to cross all obstacles to reach heavens (*Swarg*).

If the man on the death bed survives after performance of these rites, he is asked what he desires and his wish, whatever it may be, is fulfilled. If he shows no sign of improvement, a space of ground, near his charpoy or some other place, is smeared with cow dung and some grass scattered over it. In case he is on some upper floor, he is taken down to the ground floor.

A Hindu is usually not allowed to die on a bed or even on a mat, as it is supposed that the soul in separating itself from the body in which it is incorporated, enters into another body (intermediate body) which leads it to the abode of bliss destined for it, but if the dying man were to expire on a bed, he would be obliged to carry it with him, wherever he went, which evidently is very inconvenient. On the cow dung plastered ground, covered with grass, a white sheet is spread and the dying person is laid on it, with his feet to the East and his head resting on the lap of his or her eldest son or next of kin. Some Ganges water is very commonly dropped into his mouth, together with some *Tulsi* leaves. If he is a person of old advanced age, Ganges water with gold and a tiny pearl are put in his mouth, for a convenient passage to *Swarga*.

When death ensues, the eyelids are closed, cotton put into his nostrils and the body is covered with a white cloth and his face is turned towards the Ganges.

Rites after Death

If there are relatives in outstations who must attend the funeral, they are informed immediately. Obituary is also announced in the newspapers and the time of cremation is informed to all those, who may like to attend the funeral. If there are distant relations for whom waiting is necessary, then the dead body is kept surrounded by ice slabs to avoid degeneration.

After the death the eldest son or next of kin or nearer agnate, who has to perform ceremonies as the chief mourner, gets his head, beard and moustaches shaved, leaving the middle tuft of hair on the head (*Bodi*), bathes, puts on a clean loin cloth and a turban in northern regions and does not put on leather shoes for a period of 14 days. The chief mourner, in theory, is a *Brahmcharya* for the period until all the rites due to the dead are completed viz. avoid sexual intercourse, eating animal foods and drinking alcohol or intoxicating drinks. He should sleep on the ground and should not sleep for long hours. He must have two baths a day. He should have a free and pure mind to concentrate and meditate on God, day and night and pray for the peace of the soul of the departed. In some families, all brothers of the chief mourner also shave their heads but the modern times have altered this practice.

If the deceased has left a widow, she breaks off her bangles as soon as she hears about the death of her husband, removes the vermilion *Bindi* on the forehead, removes all ornaments and decoration. She loosens her hair. She is ceremonially impure and should not touch any household utensil and should sleep on ground for 14 days until she has bathed in the Ganges/ Yamuna or such holy waters. Usually few drops of water from the Ganges/ Yamuna are added to ordinary water for the bath. Water from the Ganges is normally kept in a bottle in every house of a Hindu.

While the corpse is lying inside the house, the bier (*Arṭhi*) is prepared outside. It is made of the pieces of the bed on which the deceased lay prior to his death or of bamboo of *farash* wood. Upon it is laid the hair shaved off by the next of kin together with the wife's bangles, if the deceased leaves a widow. Over the hair is spread a sheet on which the body is laid. For persons of great age or sanctity, a *Vimān* replaces the arthi.

Inside the house, the body is washed, a man's corpse being washed by men and a woman's by women. The old tradition has been that the chief mourner went with a pitcher and a rope to the nearest well, took a bath and without drying his body, he should draw water and fill up a pitcher and carry it home to wash the corpse. If the deceased was a man of high caste, a *tilak* is applied to his forehead and a sacred thread (*Janeo*) placed round his neck and a turban tied round his head. The corpse is dressed in white and a married woman, whose husband is alive, is dressed in red (*Chundri*).

A widow is also shrouded in red cloth, but no ornaments are used, whereas a woman, whose husband is alive, is decked in all her finery, a new set of bangles being put on her wrists, her teeth blackened, her eyes darkened with antimony, her nails stained with henna and a bindi fastened on her forehead.

The body is then taken out and tied to the bier. The first *Pind* (Barley-flour triangular *ladoo* made with *ghee,* by the barber's wife who carries them in a plate and the panda priest uses them when necessary) is placed on the deceased's breast. The bier is then lifted on to the shoulders of four near kinsmen of the deceased, the body being carried feet foremost. As soon as it is taken out of the door of the house, a second Pind is offered, the third offered after passing the village on the outskirts of the town and the fourth at the *Adhhmarg* or halfway between the house and the cremation ground. Before offering the fourth Pind, water is sprinkled on the ground and the bier is laid down. The first pind is replaced by the fourth. The bier is turned around, so that the head becomes foremost. The fifth pind is offered at the cremation ground. These offerings are supposed to pacify the *Yamadutas* (Messengers of God of death). When the bier is lifted from the house, by the eldest son or other near relatives, the youngers walk first and the elders behind the bier. In previous days, when sacrifice was a custom, the sacrificial animal, usually a black goat, also accompanied the mourning party. In ancient times (Vedic) as discussed later the women also accompanied to the cremation ground, but this is no more in practice.

The remaining relatives followed with their garments hanging down and their hair dishevelled, the elders in front and the youngers behind. When they reached the funeral ground, the son or brother or near relative, appointed to perform the ceremony taking a branch of the *Sami* tree, sprinkled holy water on the spot, prepared for the funeral pile, repeating the *R'Gveda* (X.14.9): "Depart ye evil spirits, slink away from here; the fathers (his departed ancestors) have made for him this place of rest."

The Cremation - The Pyre

In the Vedic Times, the ceremonies seem to have been very simple. From the 18th hymn of the 10th *Mandala* of R'Gveda, it is learnt that the dead body was, in all probability, not burnt but buried. It was deposited near a grave, dug ready for its reception, while the widow lay down or seated herself by its side, and the relatives (male and female) ranged themselves in a circle all around. Their first concern seems to have been to propitiate death, supposed to be personally present and to be naturally eager to take the opportunity of laying its hands on some other member of the family, brought by the necessity of attending the funeral within easy and somewhat tempting reach of its clutches.

Therefore the person appointed to perform the ceremony addressed Death, calling upon him to keep clear the path of the living and deprecating any attack on the survivors, who were assembled to perform pious rites for their dead relative , but had no idea of yielding themselves up into his power, or renouncing the expectation of a long life themselves. The leader of the funeral, next placed a boundary of stones between the dead body and the living relatives to mark off the limits of Death's authority. Then followed a prayer that none of those present might be removed to another world, before attaining to the age in full of a hundred years. Oblations in fire (*Yagye*) accompanied the prayer recital. Widow's married female relatives were then asked to prepare to return home. They were to lead the way without weeping or any sign of grief and without taking off their jewellery. Then the widow was told to leave the corpse of her dead husband in the inner circle assigned to Death. She, then joined her relatives in the outer circle. She was addressed in words as "Rise up, O' woman, come back to the world of living thou art lying by a dead man; come back. Thou hast sufficiently fulfilled the duty of a wife to the husband, who formerly wooed thee and took thee by the hands" (R'Gveda X. 18.8).

Further ceremony continues but before that it must be mentioned here that in R'Gveda hymn, quoted here, neither the Veda nor Manu directed or even hinted at the concremation (*Sati*) of the living wife with her dead husband. (The hymn contains the word *'Agre'*, which means 'ahead', asking other ladies to go ahead; this word has been misinterpreted as *'Agney'* which means fire and the system of Sati was justified, as if originated from the Vedas.)

Coming back to the ceremony, the performer Panda took a bow, previously placed in the hands of the deceased, and gave it to his relatives in token that the manly courage (he had displayed when alive) was not to perish with him, but to remain with his family.

The dead man was addressed thus: "I take the bow out of thy hand for our glory, and for our strength; remain thou here, we will remain here as heroes, so that in all battles, we may conquer our foes" (R'Gveda X. 18.9). The body was then tenderly committed to its 'house of clay' (R'Gveda VII.89.1) with the words, "Return to thy mother Earth, may she be kind to thee and lie lightly on thee, and not oppress thee" and with other similar words, which may be translated as:

'Open thy arms, O Earth, receive the dead
With gentle pressure and with loving welcome,
Enshroud him tenderly, even as a mother
Folds her soft vestment round the child she loves.'
(R'Gveda X. 18.11)

Lastly, columns of earth were reared over the grave. Defied ancestors and the God Yama were entreated to preserve it.

In the Post Vedic (*Greheye Sutras*) period about 5-6th centuries B.C., the funeral rites, though still conducted with much simplicity were beginning to be more elaborate and more in unison with the present custom. The practice of Cremation, doubtful in Vedic times, was now invariable, except in the case of infants and of great saints.

Funeral pile having been prepared by plastering cow dung and repeating the name of Rama seven times, the chief mourner places the body on the pile (*Chita*) and places *Panchratna* (five metals) gold, pearl, copper, silver and coral, put in the mouth of the dead. In the case of a woman, this is done at home.

The pyre should be so constructed as to lie due North and South in rectangular form. The purest wood like Sandal wood, Pipal, *Dak* are used. As Sandal wood is costly, it is rarely used, but normally a piece of sandalwood is placed on the pyre along with other wood.

When the pyre has been completed, the last fifth Pind is offered and any valuable shawl or other cloth removed from the corpse and given to sweeper or a *Maha* Brahmin. The body is then unfastened, the cords which bind it to the bier are broken with one hand and one foot and laid on the pyre. The body is laid supine upon the pyre, so that it may see the sun; its hands being placed behind and so underneath it to prevent its being cruel in the future life. The shroud is torn near the mouth and the *Panchratani* (five metals) inserted in it, while chips of sandalwood and some tulsi leaves are placed on the deceased's chest.

A man, chief mourner, then takes the burning grass in his hands and walks once right round the pyre, keeping it on his right hand, and then turns back until he reaches the feet. Here he halts and throws the burning grass on to the pyre. As soon as the fire is ablaze, all present withdraw out of reach of the smoke until the body is mainly consumed, when the chief mourner draws near again and pulling a bamboo out of the bier with it smashes the deceased's skull. He then throws the bamboo over the corpse beyond its feet. The smashing of the head skull is said to be due to the idea that the life of a man is constituted of ten elements, nine of which cease their functions at death, while the action of the tenth continues for three days after death, causing the body to swell, if it remains unhurt. The seat of this, the tenth element, is in the skull, which is accordingly smashed in order to set it free. In some regions, a cup of ghee mixed with sandalwood is poured over the smashed skull.

After this the rite of *Kar Dena* is performed, in which all those present take a piece of fuel and cast it on to the pyre. A line is then drawn with the bamboo from the head of the deceased to its feet (body being on his left). All those present stand at the end of the line and stand clasped hands and the next of the kin raise a cry of mourning. The men then disperse. The women in present days do not accompany the corpse from the house and remain in the house. In the modern days, the mourners, particularly the non relatives, assemble in a corner of the cremation ground and make speeches in reverence to the departed soul.

Then the mourners return home. If there is some sacred river nearby, they take a dip in it or else on reaching the house, they directly go to the bathroom and take a bath, change the clothes completely without touching anything in the house. The minimum, that is done in the present times is that water is sprinkled on his clothes of the person, who proceeded with the corpse, before his entry into the house.

No food is cooked in the house of the deceased on the day of his death. Nearby relatives and neighbours provide the relief. As a general rule, death is swiftly followed by cremation, but if the death takes place late in the evening or at night, then all the funeral ceremonies are postponed till the next morning and the corpse is kept indoors with a light nearby. The cremation is also delayed, awaiting the arrival of far off relatives.

After return from the cremation ground, the relatives of the deceased spread a carpet or mat on the ground publicly and sit on it whole day. Previously this carpet was laid for 14 days, but nowadays it is lifted away on 3rd-4th day. Friends and acquaintances of the bereaved family come from far and wide to sit on the carpet in order to express their grief at the death as well as to console the family. The same procedure of spreading the carpet is separately followed by women in the inner courtyard of the house. Previously the women used to beat their thighs, naked breasts and heads, but this practice has come almost to an end.

After the tenth day, the bones and ashes of the deceased are gathered together and placed in a plain undecorated funeral vase. In modern times, this act is generally performed on the fourth day and is called *Asthi Sanćaya* (Bone collection). The procedure adopted is that the chief mourner, first of all picks up three, using only his thumb and little finger. Then all those present, collect the remaining bones. The ashes are collected in a bag. The bones are kept in a vase, a hole is dug and the vessel placed in it for ten days. Simultaneously R'Gveda X. 18.10 is repeated as, "Return to thy mother Earth, the widely extended, the Broad, the Auspicious; may she be to thee like a young maiden, soft as wool; may she protect thee from the embrace of the Goddess of Corruption." The vase is generally hung on a tree or on a wall till it is taken down, wrapped in a silken cloth and sent for immersion into some sacred river, as the Ganges in Haridwar, Prayag (Allahabad), Narmada and such others. On reaching the river, the bones are cast into the river and the ceremony is performed under the guidance of the Panda, who is paid for the ceremony. The mourners, then return home with at least one bottle full of water of the Ganges called *Gangajāl.*

Kriyā Karam

It is a ceremony performed on the 11th day among Brahmins, and on 13th day of the death of the departed among other castes. It is supposed that from this moment, the departed is divested of his hideous form and assumes that of his forefathers to live among them in the abodes of bliss.

If the deceased left sons, the eldest son performs the *Kriyākaram*. The Panda (*Achārāj*) draws a square in the courtyard, showing therein the symbols of various Gods and Goddesses on the ground and constructs a *Pandal* over it. Boiled rice, flowers, vegetables and sweets as offerings are made. The kriyākaram lasts for several hours. The 13th is, in a sense, an auspicious day, auspicious that is for the performance of rites designed to secure future happiness.

A widow is made to don fine clothes and money is given to her for support in the hope that she will pass the rest of her life in resignation. Nevertheless the donors weep over her on this date. In order to ensure future fertility to the bereaved family, some vegetables and water in a new pot is brought into the house on this date.

The ceremony of installing the heir is held in the afternoon of the thirteenth day after death. On this occasion, *Pagri* (Head turban) is tied round the head of the heir/heirs. If the deceased had a shop, his heir is made to open it on this day.

13 to 17 Brahmins are feasted on this day of kriyākaram. The panda (*Achārj*) is given a bed, utensils, clothes and money according to the donor's means. All relatives and friends, who have been informed of the Kriyākaram date, come and join in the meals. Annual commemorations in respect of the dead are *Barsi* (*Barsodhi*), or first anniversary of the death. The Barsi consists in the offerings and feeding Brahmins and the poor. After this barsi, the annual commemoration is merged in the general commemoration of the dead, ensured by the observance of *Shraddh* or ancestor worship, being described later.

Death Rites of Children

As a general rule, children are buried and not burnt, if they die before attaining a certain age, which varies from place to place, viz. if the child dies of less than six months age, it is buried under a tree, and a cup of water is placed at the head of the grave. If a child over six months but under five years dies, he is buried or thrown into the water. Town people usually prefer to set the body of a child afloat on a stream, but villagers, as a rule, bury their children. Cremation of children is not unusual, it is not the rule to vouchsafe them all the rites, if they die before the age of 10 or even 14. The body of a married child, irrespective of age, is cremated. The rites at the burial or cremation of a child are very simple.

On return, after the burial/cremation of a child, it is a practice for the mourners to bring back some fresh leaves from a tree, vegetables and water and to give that in the lap of the mother of the dead child in order to ensure fertility and blessings for a continuance of family's fertility. When a child is born, after the death of one, the new born is protected against all evil eyes. He is not clad in gorgeous clothes. Milk is not fed to him in the presence of anyone, especially a woman from neighborhood. His Tonsure (*Mundan*) ceremony is done after long. Opprobrious names are given to those born afterwards viz. *Khota* Ram, Khota means ass; *Giddar Mal*, Giddar means jackal and so on, so as to distract any extra attention.

Sati System or Widow Burning

The heary history of this gruesome system has been traced by the archaeologists as far back as 12,000 years, if not more. In 1978, two double burials were discovered at Mahadaha village in Pratapgarh district of Uttar Pradesh, which antedate the system of Sati to 10,000 B.C. Whether the widows were done to death before burial or were entombed alive, has not been ascertained. The 17 excavated skeletons of the Mesolithic period belong to a tall and handsome race. On an average the men were 190 cm tall and the women 177 cm, but they had a short span of 17-35 years. Two graves had two skeletons, one each of a man and a woman. The skeletons rested side by side in one grave with the woman on the left. In the second one, the woman's skeleton lay on the man's. The skulls were resting on the left side and the microliths and shells were scattered all over the skeleton. The Harrappan civilization of Lothal, 4,500 years old, is seen to have been the votaries of a Sati system. Out of 14 skeletons exhumed, three pairs of male-female skeletons have been recovered, attesting to the fact that widows were buried with their dead husbands.

Widow sacrifice, which existed among the aboriginal, was prescribed by the Vedic Aryans. We have already referred to the fact how the word 'Agre' was misinterpreted as '*Agni*'. The first injunction against this gruesome custom is given in the R'Gveda and *Atharva* Veda. Among the aboriginal, it was a belief that a Sati's great supernatural powers, motivated others to ensure that she cared to look upon; that she could descend to hell and force the powers of the pit to yield her ancestors, relatives and friends and bring them to salvation. The belief prevailed that a man's possessions could be sent with him for use in the next world, if they were burnt or buried with him; his wife was his chief possession and his source of pleasure and had to be dispatched to serve him in his next life. The Greeks surmised that Sati system was to prevent a wife from poisoning her husband, the fact that she would have to die with him would inhibit any such intention. Another reason put forth was that the widow might misbehave and bring disgrace to the family. Supporting a widow and interest in her property, were some reasons for encouraging Sati system.

The honour given to Sati women, lured some widows to mount the pyre with the husband. In some Hindu houses, the hand-marks of women, who committed Sati, were left imprinted on walls with turmeric paste; many of these were honoured and almost delified and special 'Sati Stones', recording their virtues and fortitude, were inscribed in their honour.

Sati had become part of the Hindu ethos by convention and usage, till Raja Ram Mohan Roy revolted against it in 1818. Later the Governor General Lord William Bentinck issued a decree, before the end of 1829, which made 'Sati' or widow burning, thenceforth punishable as murder throughout British India. The efforts of Raja Ram Mohun Roy, the greatest Brahmin reformer of Modern India, were thwarted in 1987, when 28 widows reported to have mounted the pyre in Deorala in Rajasthan, whereas dozens of Sati attempts have been nullified by timely tip off to the police. However this ritualistic sacrifice of Sati is no longer practised and every effort is made to abolish it. Now there is no ban on the widows. They are not forced to undergo Sati. They can remarry and are not debarred from inheritance of property. The existing revised laws are very liberal and greater freedom has been bestowed upon the widows.

Effects of Death

Subsequent Wives: If a man loses his first wife and marries again, he places a silver effigy (*Pahajri*) of his first wife, round the neck of the second and distributes, sweetmeats among young girls in memory of the former. For the first three nights he and his wife, sleep with a naked sword between them, a custom prevalent in hilly regions of Northern India. If he loses his second wife also, he is married the third time to a plant (Tulsi) or a sheep, so that the marriage to his third wife will be his fourth and not third. His third wife wears the *pahajris* of the first two, and all other rites are also observed.

Effects on Betrothed Girl: If a girl loses her fiance, she is made to stand in the way of the funeral cortege and pass under the bier in order to avert all evil in future. In South West , especially the fiance's parents attribute his death to the girl, and her relatives perform rites to avert evil to her.

Effects on a Girl Widow: If the husband of a young girl dies, his ashes are wrapped in a cloth, which is put round the widow's neck in belief that she will pass her remaining life in patience and resignation. At present, remarriage is the rule.

Death Rites of the Old: When an old man is dying, the womenfolk of the family prostrate themselves before him and make an offering of money, which is the barber's prerequisites. If an old man dies, leaving grandsons and great grandsons, his relatives throw silver flowers and silver coins (if poor, copper coins) over his bier.

Death from Disease or Violence: If children die of small pox, their corpse is thrown into water; the idea being that the Goddess of Small Pox *Sheetla* must not be burnt or cast into fire. When thrown into the water, the body is put in a big earthen vessel full of earth and sand to sink it.

Death at Certain Times: According to the older astrology, the sky was divided into 27 lunar mansions (*Nakshatras* - constellations), of which 2 1/4 thus lay in each of the 12 radical signs (*Ras*) and of these nakshatras the last five viz., the second half of *Dhahishta*, Sat *Bikka*, *Purbabhadrapad*, *Utra bhadrapad* and *Reoti*, occupy the signs of Aquarius (*Kumbh*) and Pisces (*Min*). This period of 4 1/2 nakshatras is counted as 5 days and thence called *Panchank* or dialectically *Panjak*. This period is uncanny in several ways and it is especially inauspicious for a death, or to recall the original idea, for a cremation, to occur in it. Anyone so dying can only obtain salvation if expiatory ceremony is performed on his behalf. This consists in employing five Brahmins to recite verses, and on the 27th day after the death, on which the moon is again in the asterism in which the deceased died, the *Shanti* is performed (Expiatory ceremony), various things such as clothes, flowers and furniture being given away.

When a man dies in the Panchank, idols of *Kusha* grass, are made, one for each of the remaining days of the Panchank and burnt with the dead.

A death during a solar or lunar eclipse is considered inauspicious and in such cases *Grahan* Shanti is performed. The chief superstitions appertaining to the Panchank related, however, to the surviving kin, for the Hindus believe that a death in this period, will involve the deaths of as many others of the family, as there are days remaining in the Panchank. To avert this, the corpse should not be burnt until the Panchank is over, or if this cannot be avoided, as many dolls of cloth, as there are days remaining, are made. The dolls can be made of cow dung and in some cases, a branch of mango tree is carried with the corpse and is burnt with it.

It is not easy to say that are the precise ideas, originally underlying the Panchank observances, but it would appear as if the leading idea was that anything which occurs during this period, is liable to recur. For this reason, it is unwise to provide anything likely to catch fire—lest it gets burnt and funeral pyre ensues—during the Panchank.

Accordingly fuel should not be bought, cloth purchased or even sewn, beds be bought or houses thatched, nor should a pilgrimage be undertaken towards the south, or indeed at all, nor should one sleep with one's head towards the south. It is unlucky to undertake any new work.

Funeral Rites and Ceremonies

The funeral rites and ceremonies may originally have been designed and maintained simply to keep the ghost away. The dead are deposited and maintained simply to keep the ghost away. The dead are deposited they have gone away—they return, is ghosts, only exceptionally, and then because they have not been buried/cremated properly. The appearance of the dead in dreams or as ghosts, is interpreted, when once funeral rites have not been properly and effectually, customarily disposed off. Therefore, in funeral rites among Hindus, the offering of *Pinds* (balls of rice or flour and libations of water) is important, as a traditional customary rite.

In addition to the five pinds, offered during the actual funeral (already discussed), other Pinds, which are believed to constitute the body of the dead man, are subsequently offered. These constitute in offer of Pinds to the Brahmin for 10 days in giving him supply of uncooked food.

The thirteenth day after death, is in a sense an auspicious day, auspicious, that is for the performance of rites designed to secure future happiness. First shraddh is performed on this day with the object of:

(i) To fulfil the wishes of the deceased to feed certain persons, whom he wished to, but could not feed. So people from far and wide turn up, on receipt of information, in response to post cards posted to them with torn corners, so as to expedite delivery.

(ii) To end enmity between selves if any, to inculcate cooperation. In Uttar Pradesh (India), the serving of Mal *Pua* and *Kshir*, is the idea of instituting sweetness among all those, who turn up.

In Manu Smriti (III.237) it has been stated that the embodied *Pitris* require the periodical offering of these Pinds and water for their continual nourishment and refreshment.

Both funeral and *Sraddh* (annual commemoration) ceremonies consist in the offering of balls (Pinds), with texts and prayers, but in funeral rites, balls of rice, are for nourishment of the ghosts and for formation of a body as its vehicle, whereas in Sraddh, the Pind is said to represent the body so formed, and is offered as an act of homage to the ancestors, not necessarily connected with funerals.

CHAPTER V

Shrãddh - Ancestor Worship

Ancestor worship through *Shrãddh* is ancient. The belief in rebirth based on deeds and transmigration, though later, yet have recognized the importance of Shrãddh, as existent in ancient times. Shrãddh ceremony is highly auspicious. By this one remembers his ancestors, who were so dear to him.

A dialogue between Yudhistra and Bhima of Mahãbhãrata says that Shrãddh of the ancestors is beneficial in getting riches, popularity and sons. Gods, *Asurs*, men, *Ghandarvas*, snakes, *Rãkshasas*, devils and *Kinnars*, should worship their ancestors. Shraddh, at any time is good, but there are certain special days (discussed later).

Ancestor worship is a ritual system that has had a unifying function for extended families and clans. The cohesion of the clan undoubtedly rested wholly upon the ancestor cult. In historical times, the most fundamental belief of the Hindus, had been to ascribe power to ancestral spirits, not exclusively but predominately to the spirit of one's own ancestors.

Furthermore it was believed absolutely necessary to satisfy the spirits and win their favours by sacrifices. The ancestral cult, no doubt, helped to maintain strong ties between clan members and members, who had migrated. Periodic worship in the ancestral temple expressed and reinforced the underlying attitudes solemnly binding the kinship cult together.

The idea, that human personality continues after the

death of the body, is present in all the historical religions of the world. Individual, who acts and does things, comes to be identified with the double of the living or the ghost of the dead person, which appears in dreams. It is, therefore, the continuance of other people, rather than of oneself, after death, that is first recognized. In ancient Egypt, the continuance of the soul after death was conceived to depend on the preservation of the body (mummifying). In Christianity, the resurrection of the body is in a sense, a condition of life after death.

In historical religions, the question was as to what are the fortunes of a person after his body is dead, but was how to deal with the ghost that was apt to revisit and disturb the survivors. The question was how to induce the ghost to go away and to stay away. Funeral rites and ceremonies may originally have been designed and maintained simply to keep the ghost away.

At present, some persons believe in ghosts or visits from the dead, and others do not. Babylonians, Asyrians and Jews believe that from the other world the dead do not return. In religions, where the souls are believed to transmigrate, as among Hindus, they cannot consistently appear as ghosts. Among those religions, which believe that the dead do not return, there is no opportunity for ancestor worship. Where ancestor worship occurs, speculation as to the future state is answered before it can begin; the only aspect of the dead, which interests the living, is their activity in the affairs of the world.

Greeks and Romans, as the Chinese now, were more interested in the way in which they themselves might be affected by the spirits of their dead than they were in the fortune of the departed or the nature of their abode. They, therefore, placed all the things in the grave, which the dead may need so that the dead may have no need to return. In China, the whole house in which the death takes place is now formally and ceremoniously abandoned which was originally abandoned altogether. The idea was to deprive the deceased of any excuse for returning. The offerings made were for the ghosts to go away as sacrifices were made to Gods in the fear of calamity and to provide against it.

In due course, the community has grown into the custom of expecting the powers, whom it approaches, not only to avert calamity but to confer positive blessings. Thus from the ancestors of any particular family, that family may come to expect benefits from the beings that it worships. Offerings to Gods are made with a view to get substantial and real benefits, but the offerings to the ancestors are made in filial piety much more than the hope of personal gain.

Ancestor worship is a duty, ranking next to the worship of Gods, and it is disinterested so far as disinterestedness is possible to human nature. This is the underlying idea of Shrāddh, a custom observed by Hindus since times immemorial.

The principle underlying the offering of *Pinds* (balls of boiled rice) in Shrāddh to the three ancestors (father, grandfather and great grand father) is that for 50-100 years. The essence of the Pinds of rice, is consumed through the ethereal waves by the ancestors in their ethereal bodies. *Yageya Valkiye Smriti* (1.269) *Markāndey Purāna* (29.38), *Agni* Purāna (163.41.42) and *Mātasey* Purana (19.11-12) state that Pinds offered in Shraddh, being self contented, award life, satisfaction, wealth, knowledge, heavens (*Swarg*) and salvation to their family men.

Matasey Purāna (19.3-9) states that father, grandfather and great grandfather, according to the Vedas, have been recognized as equivalent to *Rudras* and *Adityas*. They carry these to the ancestors, when accompanied by the recitation of the names, *gotras* (Sub-caste), hymns and offerings.

According to *B'rhm* Purāna, whatever is given to the

Brahmins in Shrāddh in reverence to the ancestors, at proper time, place and character in accordance with proper rites is called Shrāddh. *Mitākashara* Yageya (1.217) has defined Shrāddh as, 'In reverence to ancestors and for their benefit, voluntarily and happily, whatever is sacrificed; anything or a liquid in relation to them,' is called Shrāddh.

Origin of Shrāddh

The composers of *Dharamashāstras* have explained the importance of Shraddh from *Sutra Kaal* (600 B.C.) to the medieval times. *Aapstambh Dharmasutra* (2.7.16.1-3) states, "In ancient times, the men and the Gods lived in this world. The Gods, because of *yageyas*, went into the heavens (Swarg), but men remained behind. Those men, who perform yageyas, like Gods, go and live in Swarg, along with Gods. *B'rhma*, seeing the men left behind, invoked the custom of Shrāddh, which takes the men to ultimate bliss (salvation and happiness). In these ancestors are the deities. In this Brahmins, who are fed, in the presence of fire (Agni), are recognized as equivalent to God Agni. Thus feeding the Brahmins in Shrāddh, is an utmost primary action."

B'rhm Purāna (*Apodhghat Pada* 9-15. 10-99) recognizes Manu, as the pioneer of Shrāddh. *Viśnu* Purāna (3.1.30), *Vāyu* Purāna (44.38) and *Bhagwat* (3.1.22) have recognized them as Shrāddh *Dev* (God). Likewise Mahābhārata (*Shanti Parva* 345.14-21) and Viśnu *Dharamottar* (1.139.14-16) have attributed the origin of Shrāddh ceremony to the times of *Vrāha* incarnation of Viśnu, and that the Pinds offered to father, grandfather and great grandfather, should be considered as offered to God Viśnu. Thus it is clear that the Shraddh ceremony custom was initiated many centuries before the Christ and that it is as old as Manu, the father of mankind.

The term 'Shrāddh' does not occur in the Vedas, but has been referred as *Pind Pitri* Yageya (observed in

Chaturmas or *Saak megh*) and *Ashtaka Kato Upanishad* (1.3.17) mentions the word 'Shrāddh'. The one, who proclaims this in the assembly of the Brahmins, obtains immortality. So when there was an increase in the deeds done in honour of the ancestors, the word Shrāddh came into general practice. There is a deep intimacy between the words Shrāddh and *Srāddha* (veneration), according to definitions given in B'rhm Purana, *Marichi* and *Brihaspati*.

The donor, performer of Shrāddh, has an utter belief in the fact that whatever is given in Shrāddh to the Brahmins, it reaches his ancestors. *Skanda* Purāna (6.218.3) states that it has been termed Shrāddh, because in this ceremony, reverence (veneration) is fundamental. Mārkandey Purāna (29.27) pronounces that whatever is offered in Shrāddh, changes into such forms, which the ancestors, according to actions (deeds) and transmigration doctrine, gets in their new body.

Before *Shatpath Brahamana*, there was a system of performance of five yageyas by every householder viz.: *Bhoot* yageya, *Manush* Yageya, Pitri Yageya, Dev Yageya and B'Rhm Yageya. In Shatpath Brahamana and *Taitreye Aranayaka* (2.10) it is stated that *Ahvik* yageya, Pitri Yageya, Dev Yageya and B'rhm Yageya. In Shatpath Brahamana and Taitreye Arānayaka (2.10) it is stated that Ahvik yageya (in which food and water is given to the ancestors) is called Pitri Yageya.

Manu (3.70) has defined Pitri Yageya as *tarpan* (contentment of the ancestors by offerings and libation of water). Manu (3.83) has advised that every day, food and water, milk, vegetables and fruits should be offered, as Shraddh to the ancestors.

Mahābhārata gives an instance that in ancient times, *mahrishi* Atri Mahābhārata gives an instance that in ancient times, mahrishi Atri was created by B'rhma. Datātareye was born in his family. Mini was his son, of whom Shriman was the son. He underwent asceticism for thousands of years and then died. His father Nimi was grief stricken. Her performed all rites ceremoniously at the time of his death. On the 14th day of his death, Mini collected all material for the Shrāddh of his son. Next day, on 15th, *Amāvaseye* day, forgetting his sorrow, he performed Shraddh, observing all rites. Whatever articles were dear to his son, were procured and served to the Brāhmins. On the amāvaseye day, he invited seven Brāhmins, paid homage to them and served them with the food, etc.

Shrāddh is normally performed in respect to ancestors, but Nimi observed it in respect of his son, so he was depressed on account of deviating from an ancient religious custom. His mentor, *Maharshi* Atri consoled him and explained the rite of Shrāddh, as having been originated from God Brāhma. According to that the first part of Shrāddh is devoted to Agni by virtue of which evil doers (Rakshasas, *Asuras*) go away from the site of the Shrāddh. Next offering is to the father then to the grandfather and the last to the great grandfather, pronouncing their names. He explained that the ancestor worship should preferably be done on the banks of a holy river.

Brihit Prashar (P 153) has opined that on some occasions the rite of Shrāddh may not be strictly observed. Boudhāyan and Vridshatatappa (Smriti *Chandrika* 337) has permitted the performance of this rite for anyone, out of love and affection, thus allaying the fears of Nimi. As we shall see later, some kinds of Shrāddh, permit the performance of ceremony in respect to anyone.

Time and Place

Time and place are important factors in the due performance of Shrāddh. The time: the month of *Bhadra* (September-October) and especially the *Krishna Paksha* (dark moonlit) and *Ashwin* (October) are believed to be the most auspicious. Benefits derived from the performance of Shrāddh on different days are as under:

First day awards beautiful wife, who produces handsome and capable children.

Second day produces many girls.

Third day observance gets horses.

Fourth awards many small animals to the house.

Fifth begets many sons.

Sixth increases beauty in the house.

Seventh increases production in the fields.

Eighth develops trade and business.

Ninth results in increase of horses, mules, cows and such other hoofed animals.

Tenth day performance results in the increase of cows.

Eleventh begets clothes, utensils and birth of enlightened sons.

Twelfth increases food, silver and riches.

Thirteenth gets honour and reputation among friends and relatives.

Fourteenth results in early death of his relatives and the donor has to enter a war soon. This day is unlucky.

Fifteenth *amāvaseya* day fulfils all desires of the donor. All days in Krishna Paksha (dark fortnight) from tenth to fifteenth day except the fourteenth are auspicious days for the observance of Shrāddh.

Place for the performance of Shrāddh can be any place, according to the convenience of the donor, but there are certain places, which are considered more auspicious. At Benaras, the *ghat* near the pool of Mani Karnika, is a very suitable one. The Brāhmin invited to perform the ceremony constructs a small altar (*Vedi*). Then taking a number of small earthenware platters or saucer he arranges them round the sand, putting Til (Sesamums) seeds in one, rice in another, honey in the third, areca or betel nut in the fourth and *Chandan* (Sandalwood) in the fifth. Next he takes flour of wheat or barley and kneads that into one large Pind, rather smaller than a cricket ball, which he carefully deposits in the centre of the sand altar, scattering over it jasmine flowers, *Khaskhas* grass and wool are placed. On one side of it a betel leaf, with areca nut and a single copper coin are placed. Then having poured water from a jug, into his hands, he sprinkles it over all the offerings, arranged in the manner described above.

Other similar operations follow. An earthenware platter, containing a lighted wick, is placed near the offerings, then other platters are filled with water, which are all poured over the Pind; another small platter with a lighted wick is added to the first, then some milk is placed in another platter and poured over the *Pinda*; then once more water is sprinkled over the Pinda, Finally the Brahmin folds his hands together and pays homage to the Pinda, representative of ancestors, reciting the mantras (hymns).

During all this time, the man for whose parents, it is performed, continues to repeat mantras and prayers under the directions of the Brāhmin, quite regardless of the noise and his surroundings. The ceremony is completed with the feeding of the Brahmin.

The efficacy of the Shrāddh performed is that wherever in their progress onwards departed relatives may have arrived, the Shrāddh takes them without further impediment or delay to Vishnu's heaven (*Baikuntha*).

Pinds offered at Gayā are considered as the most auspicious. From the place of Shrāddh, *Rakshasa* and other evil doers should be removed. People clad in earthen red coloured clothes, lepers, depraved, murderers of Brāhmins and irreligious relatives should be removed away from the place of the Shrāddh. The day and time for the performance of the Shrāddh, is of great importance and great stress has been laid by different *Rishis* and saints on this aspect of the

Shrāddh. Gautam (15.1-2) states that in olden times, Shrāddh was performed on Amavāseye.

Aapstambh *Dharma* Sutra (2.7.16.4-7) has advocated that the Shrāddh should be performed in the later half of every month, later days in later half should be given importance. Gautam (15.3) and Vashishta (11.16) have advised that Shrāddh should be performed on any day in *K'rsna Paksh* except the fourth and fourteenth.

Manu (3.276 - 278) has advised the performance of Shraddh on any day from tenth onwards in dark moonlit fortnight, except the fourth, but if it is performed on the tenth or eleventh and under *Bharni* and *Rohini* constellations, then the Shrāddh fulfills all wishes of the donor, but if anyone performs it on the eleventh or thirteenth and under *Kritika*. *Mrigshira* constellations, then he obtains lucky progeny. K'rsna fortnight constellations, then he obtains lucky progeny. K'rsna fortnight has been given superiority over *Shukl* Paksh (moonlit night).

Yegeyvalkeye Smriti (1.217-218), *Kurum* Purāna (2.20, 2-8), *Mārkandeye* Purāna (28.20) and Vrāha Purāna (13.33-35) have given the days for Shraddh as:

Auspicious days are Amāvaseye and *Ashtmi* (15th and 8th) in K'rsna fortnight, when the sun starts moving towards the North or the South; receipt of gifts of food; arrival of any wise Brāhmin, the arrival of the sun on the equatorial line, the day when the Sun moves from one constellation to another, etymological, astrological evening called *Gaj Chhaya*, Lunar or Solar eclipse or when the donor has an utter desire.

Gargeye Prashar *Madhaveye* (1.2.324) have advised that Shrāddh should not be performed on *Nanda* Friday, 3rd of K'rsna fortnight birthday constellation and one day before it and in later constellations, because there is liable to be a loss of sons and wealth. In Mahābhārata (*Anushāsan* Parva), it has been stated that anyone, who performs

Shrāddh on third of the month, he gains a place of importance among the ancestors, but young ones in his family die early.

Vishnu *Dharama* Sutra (77.1-7) has stated that when the Sun moves from one constellation to another, both the days (*Uttarāyan* and *Dakshināyan*), etymologically, the constellation of the donor, the day of the birth of the sons, are all days of *Kamey* (desirability) and that *yageye* (Shrāddh) performed on these days, gives utmost happiness to the ancestors. Vishnu Dharama Sutra (78.1-7) states that the Shrāddh performed on a Sunday, makes the donor free from diseases for all times. Those, who perform Shrāddh on Monday, Tuesday, Wednesday, Thursday, Friday or Saturday get reputation, victory in war, fulfilment of wishes, high knowledge, wealth and long age respectively.

Agni Purāna (117.61) states that Shrāddh done on pilgrimage gives imperishable contentment to the ancestors.

Aapstambh Dharma Sutra (7.17.23-25) Manu Smriti (3.280); Vishnu Dharama Sutra (77.8.9) and *Bhavisheye* Purāna (1.185.1) have prohibited the performance of the Shrāddh in the night, evening or when the Sun just rises, but the time of Lunar eclipse is an exception to this rule.

Different Kinds of Shrāddh

In ancient India, only three ceremonies were observed in reverence to the ancestors.

1. Pind Pitri Yageya: Monthly yageya (*Aashvlayan Greh* Sutra (215.10).

2. *Maha* Pitri Yageya: This was performed in *Chetra* (Mar-April) or *Magh* (Saak Magh-Dec-January).

3. Ashtaka Shrāddh: This was performed on the eighth day after full moon (*Purnimā*). Gautam (8.19) has divided this into seven *paak* yageyas and forty *sanskaras* (Sacraments). It has great importance and there is no difference of opinion about its days, months, governing

deities, offerings and rituals.

Pavaran Shrāddh: It is of great importance, because its ritual has been recognized as the ritual for other *ashtkas* (Shrāddh). *Shathpath* Brāhamana (2.4.2) describes the Pind Pitri yageya (Pavaran Shrāddh ritual) in details. When the moon is not seen in the East or the West, then that donor offers food to the ancestors every month. He performs this in the afternoon. Sitting before the fire, facing the South and putting the sacred thread on his left shoulder, he gets the eatables unladen from the carriage. Then standing North South and facing South, he removes the husk form the paddy. He cleanses the rice only once. Then he boils the rice, standing Southwards, he puts *ghee* (clarified butter).

Moving away, he makes two offerings to the fire (Agni), in order to please Gods and then by their permission, he offers food to his ancestors. The two oblations are to Gods Agni and Soma. The oblation to Agni is with the recitation of *Svaha* mantra and recites, "Svāha to Soma, who lives with the ancestors."

Then he places the spoon on the fire. Next he draws a line towards the South, which compensates the absence of the altar. Then he places the fire at the end of the Southern line. If this is not done, then the Asuras or Rakshasas will make the food impure. Simultaneously he recites, "Asuras, small or big, in any form, disturbed ;by oblations to the ancestors and roaming here and there, May Agni flee them away." Then he lifts up the pot of water and washes the hands of the ancestors, pronouncing the names of the father, grandfather and great grandfather. This is done in the same way, as is done for the guests.

Then he offers three Pinds of rice to the ancestors and says, "This is for you," gives it to the father of the donor and says, "O' ancestors, enjoy this and partake your share." Then facing South, he gets aside. He should hold his breath and stand still. He, then turns left and says, "The ancestors are satisfied and have occupied their own places." Then pouring water on the Pinds, he requests ancestors to wash hands, requesting each by name. Pulling downwards his dress, he salutes the ancestors six times. This act is very dear to the ancestors, because the seasons are six and the ancestors are the seasons. He says, "O' Fathers; give us home," because ancestors are the rulers of the house. Then Pinds are placed separately in a broad dish and the donor smells them, because smelling is the part of the donor and puts the fire (at the end of the Southern line), into the fire of the yageya (*Baajsnayee Samhita* 2.30,2.31).

Ekodidasht Shrāddh: It is only a modification of Pavaran Shrāddh, the only difference being that there are three ancestors in Pavaran, whereas there is only one in this Shrāddh. Only one oblation is given in this and that very one is purifying. Only one Pind is offered. Brāhmins are not invited to this. This Shrāddh is of three kinds; Nava on the 10th-11th day; *Navamisr* from 11th day of the death up to one year and still later is Purana.

Abhyudeepak Shrāddh: This Shrāddh is completed on *Manglik* occasions,. Brāhmins are invited in even numbers. The performance is from right to left. Barley is used instead of Til (Sesamums). *Uprark* (514) declares this Shrāddh as an amended form of Pavaran. Same rites are observed. On auspicious occasions, *Nandi* Shrāddh and *Brihadi* Shrāddh are performed, which are miniature forms of this Shrāddh.

Mahalaya Shrāddh: This is a famous popular Shrāddh mentioned in the *Purānas*. K'rsna Paksh (fortnight) of *Aswin-Bhadrapada* (Sept.-October) is specific for this Shrāddh and can be performed on any day from first to fifteenth (Amāvaseye). The rites are according to Pavaran Shrāddh. If this may not be possible, then all rites of Pavaran Shrāddh may be observed, except praise, oblations and offering of Pinds. The presiding deities of this Shrāddh are *Dhuri* and *Lochana*. This Shrāddh is not only for male ancestors, but also for female ancestors and other relatives and their consorts. It should not be observed in *Malmas*.

Other Shrāddhas: Shrāddhs mentioned above viz. Pavaran, *Ekadidasht*, *Abhiyudayik*, and Mahalaya are rarely performed in these days, but *Matameh* Shrāddh, *Dehhitr Pratipada* Shrāddh and *Ashidhavanvami* Shrāddh are performed, even nowadays. Dehhitr Pratipada Shrāddh is performed by one (whose parents are alive) in reverence to his grand maternal uncle, on the first of *Shukl* Paksh (Moonlit fortnight) in the month of Aswin (October). Previous wearing in of sacred thread is not necessary.

Abhidhavnavami Shrāddh is performed in respect of one's mother or other married ladies, in the month of *Bhadrapad* Aswin (Sept.-October) on the ninth day of K'rsna Paksh. It is stopped, when the husband of the dead married lady dies.

Sanghat Shrāddh is performed in respect many members dying on one and the same day, as in a boat disaster.

Jeev Shrāddh, own Shrāddh, while still alive, is mentioned in Boddhāyan. It can be performed by anyone for his own welfare, even when his successor is alive. Another person performs this with the recitation of *R'Gveda* hymn 10.16.9.

In the modern times, many changes have been made in the performance of Shrāddhs and are more dependent on the Brāhmins. Steel utensils have been brought into use for cooking, as against brass and bronze ones; but still fundamental elements of Shrāddh are observed religiously.

Who can perform Shrāddh

Vishnu Dharamottar Purāna states that those who obtain the property of the dead, should perform Shrāddh. Also those who are capable of performing Shrāddh, as successors, can perform Shrāddh, and are authorized to get the property of the dead. *Gobhil Smiriti* (3.70; 2.104) a sonless mother on death, should not be offered Shrāddh by the husband or by the father in respect of his son or by an elder brother in respect of his younger brother. As stated earlier, Nimi performed Shrāddh in respect of his dead son, but later on repented, having gone against religious customs. *Vrihatprashar* (153) has justified it as that such an ordinary rule may have to be overlooked, under exceptional circumstances. However, Boddāyan and Vrihadshatatap (Smiriti Chandrika 337) state that a Shrāddh, particularly at Gaya, can be performed in reverence to anyone, out of veneration and affection. A grandson can also perform Shrāddh according to *Mitakshara.*

Brāhmin for a Shrāddh: While in charitable yageye or performance, no discrimination of Shrāddh, it is essential that a proper choice of the Brāhmin should be made, according to clan, knowledge, modesty, condition, beauty and his heritage. Brāhmins are either *Panktidooshak* or *Panktipavan.*

Panktidooshak Brāhmins are gamblers, abhortionists, TB patient, cowherd, illiterate, village announcer, interest receiver (money lender), singer, seller of all type of things indiscriminately, intruder into the house of others, poison giver, consumer of grains of criminals, seller of wines, Occupational palmist, Government servant, seller of oils, false evidence giver, quarrelsome with father, receiver of adulterer in his house, blemish, thief, occupational sculptors, imposter, backbiter, friend cheater, women chaser, teacher of *Shudras,* occupational manufacturer of arms and ammunition, roamer with dogs, one bitten by a dog, who is a bachelor but his younger brother has been married, skin diseased, lover of Guru's consort, blind, acrobat, one who lives on the earnings of the temple and an occupational astrologer.

Such panktidooshak Brāhmins should not be invited

to perform Shrāddh ceremony, because the food consumed by them goes to devils (Rakshasas). There are different type of curses, described in Mahābhārata (Anushasan parva), which befall a donor, because of feeding such panktidooshak Brāhmins.

Shrāddh is not the occasion for widening friendship, therefore friends should not be invited to a Shrāddh. Shrāddh food should not be given to friends or enemies, but should be given to natural persons only. Food given to friends or enemies does not reach the ancestors.

Instead of feeding hundreds, it is worthwhile feeding one capable Brāhmin. An inter-caste Brāhmin and a Brāhmin born out of wedded woman for second time, is not suitable, because everything given to such is equal to ashes.

Oblations (Offerings): Any woman from another caste should not be employed on cooking food for the Shrāddh. A woman under menstruation or a woman with crippled ears should not be allowed at the site of the Shrāddh yageya.

The seven great Shraddh yageya deities are: B'Rhma, Pulsateya, Vashishta, Pulha, Angira, Ritu and Mehrishi Kashyap. While offering *Pindas, Gāyatri* Mantra should be recited, as well as '*Sanate Outrnatey Swaha*' should be enchanted. Different type of ingredients in the food award different bliss. Til (Sesamums) award the maximum. They should be used in the food, as also be sprinkled at the site of the Shrāddh yageye.

Sesamums, rice, black gram (*Urad*), water, fruits and vegetables, award satisfaction to the ancestors for one month. According to Manu, a Shrāddh, in which maximum use of the sesamums is made, is perennial.

Kshir (boiled rice in milk) mixed with Ghee (clarified butter) awards contentment to the ancestors for one year.

Any edibles, offered to the ancestors, when mixed

with honey, give limitless satisfaction to the ancestors.

Ingredients which should not be included in the food for the Shrāddh are *Heeng* (Asafoetida), *Lassan* (Garlic) and onions. Forbidden vegetables are Drum stick, *Kachnar*, carrots, pumpkin, *Amla* and squash gourd (*konhadda*).

Black salt, black *zeera*, *veerya* salt, *Sheetpak saag*, bamboo tendrils and *singhara* (water potato) are prohibited. All sorts of salt, *Jaman* fruit, food spoiled by tears of the mourners, should not be consumed in Shrāddh. *Sudarshan* saag (leafy) has also been forbidden, because it gives no pleasure to Gods and the ancestors. The ancestors, satisfied and contented, with the offerings and oblations, award life, riches, knowledge and salvation to the successors.

To end with the topic of Shrāddh, in reverence to the *Pitras* (ancestors), we narrate here answers to certain queries raised between a dialogue of Bhishma and Yudhishtra of the Mahābhārata in relevance to Shrāddh.

Any person, who is a donor and the Brāhmin who performs Shrāddh ceremony should not enter into intercourse with wife: the donor for one month because from the day of the Shrāddh, the Pitras (ancestors) live in his semen for one month. The Brāhmin concerned, on the day of the performance of the Shraddh, is recognized as the ancestor of the donor on that day. So he should not have intercourse with his wife on that day, because that day, his wife is equivalent to another's (donor's) wife.

In reply to a second query, ancestors and Gods replied that the importance of three Pinds is that the first pinda should be put in water, because that Pind, inside water, gratifies the Moon and the Moon, itself being a God, satisfies the ancestors. The 2nd Pind should be fed to the wife of the donor, because by blessings of the ancestors, that pind will bestow sons to the desirous donor husband. The 3rd pind put in the fire (Agni), satisfies the ancestors by virtue of which they fulfill all wishes of the donor.

In another query about the action, which one should

perform in order to gain the blessings of the ancestors, the later replied that by donation of a blue bull, oblations of sesamum mixed water and by offer of lighted lamp, one (donor) gets rid of the debt of the ancestors. So any donation given disinterestedly is great imperishable and ever gives satisfaction to the ancestors. Such donors will save their ancestors from going to hell (*Naraka*). Thus the time, action, ritual, performer and fruit of Shrāddh, were described in Anushasan *Parava* of the Mahabharata.

CHAPTER VI

Hindu Pregnancy and Childbirth Rites

IN NO country of the world are domestic religion and sacredotalism so curiously associated together and carried to such extremes as in India. The actual religious lives of a large number of Hindus, pious and earnest minded, are still careful to impress a religious character on every act and circumstance of their domestic life. His religion is bound up in the bundle of his everyday existence. His religion is an affair of family usage, domestic ritual and private observances. Sacredotalism exerts a strong power over family religion as on congregational religion in other countries. Action of the priestly caste commences with the first moment of his unconscious existence as a living organism. From that to death and even after death, every Hindu is held to be the lawful property of the priests, who exact fees for innumerable ceremonies performed on his behalf. Every village has first its religious teacher (Guru) who teaches Vedic *Gayatri* to the desirous and secondly the ceremonial priest, who serves as a domestic *Purohit*. The priest is guided and bounded by a complicated religious code, as an intricate civil code to the lawyer.

First menstruation after marriage

The first menstruation, after the marriage has been consummated, is the occasion of strict taboo. The wife must not touch anyone and should not even see anyone to secure which, she is shut up in a dark room in hilly areas. She must not use milk, oil or meat and while she is still impure. The rite observed is on a day chosen to be auspicious by a Brahmin, all the female relatives of the wife assemble and kinswomen wash her head. Then after she has bathed, five cakes of flour with some fruit are placed on her lap with a pretty child, in order that she may herself bear a child so beautiful. Looking into the face, she gives it some money and cakes, and then the family priest makes her worship *Ganapati* (*Ganesa*). The priest gets his fees and the women spend the night in singing. The offerings made to the God are also given to the Brāhmin priest.

Pregnancy: General observances

The pregnant women should not go near a dead body, even of a near relative. She should not cross a stream, especially in the evening, lest the water spirit exerts an evil influence on her, nor should she visit a woman newly delivered. In all these cases, the danger feared is abortion from the influence of evil spirits. If a snake appears and tries to escape, the people believe that the shadow of a pregnant woman falling on it, will cause it to crawl slowly.

During pregnancy, the parents are both peculiarly susceptible to the effects of an eclipse, and it is safest for the wife to keep to her bed and not see the eclipse, but the father is not under any such binding. During eclipse, application of antimony by the wife to her eyes and the putting of *tilak* by the husband should be avoided lest the child be so marked. Extremists believe that locking and unlocking should be avoided lest the fingers of the child to be born be bent and become powerless. If the wife cuts any wood with an axe or breaks anything such as a piece of wood, the fingers of the child will be marked. Anything, such as stamping or printing done during an eclipse is liable to leave an impression on the child's body.

To avert ill luck on a child or from his birth during an eclipse practice in vogue is that an image in gold, connected with the asterism, in which the eclipse occurred (solar or lunar), together with the image of *Rahu* are reverenced. A *hawan* (*Agni jageye*) is also performed. The particular type of wood—AK wood for solar and *Plas* wood for lunar eclipse are used in the *yageye*. Like other unlucky children, a child born under the eclipse is weighed every month, on the *Sankrant* (October-November) day, against seven kinds of grains, all of which is given away in charity.

Antenatal Period (Before Birth)

If a woman's children all die, she procures, in the third month of her pregnancy, a piece of iron, taken out of a sunken boat, and from it has a manacle made. This she wears on her right leg, and it is believed to prevent her future children's premature death. In the third month of first pregnancy, dried dates, pieces of coconut, loaves of wheat flour fried in *ghee* are given to the pregnant mother, sent by her mother, of which she eats a little and the rest is distributed among her kinsmen and the brotherhood. Both husband and wife put on new clothes and worship family God. In most of the cases, the mother also sends clothes for the husband and her daughter.

At the fifth month, a similar ceremony is observed and the mother of the wife also sends sweets (nourishing rich flour *ladoos* baked in ghee) clothes and some money.

At the commencement of the seventh month, the husband's parents celebrate. First of all, the wife's parents send her new clothes, a coconut, dried dates and money together with a present of clothes to her husband's parents, who on their part present her with new clothes. On a lucky day chosen by the Brahmin, the husband and the wife, dressed in new clothes, sit side by side and revere images of the gods, drawn by the Brahmin on the floor. The husband's mother then places a coconut and dried dates in the wife's lap and congratulations are exchanged. Huge loaves of flour fried in ghee are then distributed among the brotherhood.

Usually when a wife is pregnant for the first time, she is sent to her parent's house in the seventh month and presented with a lump of jaggery, as an intimation to them of her condition. Her parents give her clothes for herself, her husband and his mother, and other presents with which she returns to her husband's house. On the rising of the new moon in the seventh month, a Brahmin is called in, and the husband and the wife are seated side by side with their kinsmen. A jar is then filled with water and a lamp filled with ghee put over it and lighted. The Brahmin makes an idol of Ganapati out of flour, and worships their ancestors. A small gold ornament, presented by her parents, is hung round the wife's neck, which is eventually given to the child when born.

Abortion

If abortion has ever occurred, or is feared for the woman, wizards prevent it by giving her (1) a piece of wood from a scaffold on which a man has been hanged or (2) copper coins, which have been thrown over the bier of an old man (3) a tiger's flesh or claw. The idea, in each of these charms, is to increase the vitality or prolong the life of the child.

Child birth

Premature birth. Birth in the eighth month of pregnancy is attributed to a cat having entered the mother's room in a former confinement. A child born in this month will, it is believed, die on the eighth day, in the eighth month or eighth month or eighteenth year after birth. Hence the number eight is never mentioned while speaking of the child's age.

Lucky and unlucky births

The planets, months and days have their influence on both of the children. There are various superstitions and beliefs about unlucky ones and various remedies are practiced in different parts of India. Some are described here.

Monday is an unlucky day for birth, and as a remedy the child's nose or ear is bored.

Saturn: Seven kinds of grain, or anything black, such as iron or a black buffalo, should be given in charity.

Mars: Articles such as copper, *Gur* (jaggery), cloth dyed red, oil should be given in charity.

The Sun: Reddish things, such as Ghee, gold, wheat, a red coloured cow should be given in charity.

The Moon: White articles, such as silver, rice, a white cow, white cloth are the articles to be given.

Mercury and Venus: Green articles such as mung (green gram), green clothes or fruits such as oranges.

Jupiter: Yellow things such as yellow clothes, gram pulse, yellow sweetmeats, gold, etc. are the remedies.

Rah (ascending node): coconut, ghee, sugar and Urd (pulse).

Kret (Typhoon: the descending node): *Samosa* (a fried product) and bluish clothes are given in charity.

Above mentioned charity is given in worship of planets and is called *Greha Puja*.

The planets governing different days are—Monday (Moon), Tuesday (Mars), Wednesday (Mercury), Thursday (Jupiter), Friday (Venus), Saturday (Saturn).

Under natal astrology, the following thirteen *Nakshatras* are unlucky for child birth:

1. *Asauni*
2. *Rawati* (*Reoti*)
3. *Maghan* (*Magha*)
4. *Shelkhan*
5. *Mulan* (*mul*)
6. *Jeshtan* (*Jeshtha*)
7. *Garhan* (eclipse)
8. *Atepat*
9. *Shankrant*
10. *Gand*
11. *Chaudas* (14th)
12. *Amavas* (15th)
13. *Bhadra*

The 4th in the Shelkhan, *Jeyestha* and *Rewati* asterisms and the first in Mulan, *Ashwini* and Maghan are called *Gands*. A birth in these is unlucky. If it occurs by day, it is unlucky for the father, if by night for the mother and if in the morning or evening for the child itself. These are the unlucky days under these nakshatras in the dark half of the lunar month. A child born on any of these days bodes ill to the parents. But all these refinements are unknown to the popular astrology and the popular practice is to regard births in Jeshtan, Mulan, *Ashlekhan* and Maghan asterism as unlucky.

The remedy prescribed is that the father of the child must not see the child until, in the recurrence if the *nakshatra* in which it was born, he has worshipped the Gods or until five dolls have been made and put in a copper vessel and anxiously propitiated. A perforated jug is allowed to trickle water over the heads of the parents. Charity is given to Brahmins. The evil influence of birth in the dark night (*K'rsna paksh*), Chāudas (fourteenth day) or Amāvas (last day of the dark half) is that the children born on the former day are not propitious to the mother, those born on the latter to the father. To avert their evil influence, an idol of Śiva is made of silver or otherwise, in an earthen jar with leaves from trees like mango, *Palas*, *Pipul*, Bel etc., is covered with a red cloth, on which a coconut is placed. On that the idol of Śiva is placed, duly purified with mantras. Hawan (*Yagaye*) is performed. The idol is given to the Brāhmin or else money in lieu.

Children born in *Kartik* (Oct-Nov) is inauspicious and is liable to misfortunate others and themselves. Various rites are performed to avert the consequence of their births. The parents must bathe with water drawn from seven wells and mixed with turmeric, sandal, ginger and other drugs. Water from seven wells or rivers is purified with mantras. Such water is poured on the mother and the child through a sieve. Charity is given. A child born, when the moon is in the sixth or eighth zodiacal sign, is ill omened. To avert its evil influence on the 27th day of such birth, rice, camphor, a gold/silver piece, piece of white cloth are given in charity. This is an orthodox rite and is not popularly observed.

The first born

The first born child is of great importance and every care is taken of the mother in her antenatal period and at the time of the birth of the child. This, particularly in case of the birth of a son, is an occasion for great rejoicing. The families undertake pilgrimage in gratitude. Sacrifice, offerings and feasts are given at the shrines. A son is to every Hindu the first and the last of all necessary he desires. Through a son, he pays his own father the debt, he owes him for his own life, and secures similar payments for the gift of life bestowed by himself. Aitreya Brāhman of the *R'GVeda* (VII.5.13) says, "When a father sees the face of a living son, he pays a debt in him, and gains immortality. The pleasure, which a father has in his son, exceeds all other enjoyments. His wife is a friend, his daughter an object of compassion, his son shines as his light in the highest world." Manu (VII.3) says, "A man is perfect, when he consists of three - himself, his wife and his son." Yajnavalkaye says, "Immortality in future worlds and heavenly bliss are obtained by means of sons, grandsons and great grandsons."

On the eleventh day of the birth of the first born, alms are given to the poor. Brāhmins and kinsmen are feasted. Menials receive gifts. In previous days, if a child was born to parents, who have long been without offspring and those who had taken a vow, the first born was sacrificed in the name of the small pox Goddess (*Shitala*), this practice is now a cognizable crime and exits no more.

If the first born of one sex, after three of the other

sex, was considered unlucky and its birth portends (1) the death of a parent (2) loss of wealth (3) fire to the house of birth and (4) some other calamity such as snake bite, disaster by lightning.

A boy born after three girls is considered unlucky, but not if a girl is born after three boys. Various remedies and ceremonies are held to avert the ill effects of one born after three, and are usually the same as are observed to avert the evil effects of one born under an evil nakshatra. A horse shoe, painted with vermilion, is burnt on the third or tenth day after the birth of such a child. It is attached to the bed of the mother. This is one of the superstitious remedies among others.

The Eighth child

The eighth child is very unlucky. If a son, he is liable to cause his father's death. In some regions, eighth is considered dangerous to the mother. The remedy is to pass a spinning wheel (*Charkha*) thrice round the mother and give it to the midwife. Although Krisna's birth was also eighth, but that was a divine birth, for the benefit of the human beings, therefore his birth cannot be compared with that of the ordinary human beings, for whom the eighth birth is considered unlucky.

Twins

There is no objection to the birth of twins; but if a boy and a girl are born as twins, it is considered unlucky in the hilly areas. Different classes have different ideas about twins. Some consider them a good omen, while others think that they forbade ill luck. Women do not consider their birth an evil and they have a proverb that a woman who gives birth to twins, goes straight to paradise on her death. Regarding the birth of the twins, there are different notions - (i) if air gets in during the intercourse, it splits the seed into two and gives birth to twins (ii) if a woman cuts a fruit, which has grown in a pair, that pregnant woman will give birth to twins.

Teething

If a child first teethes from its upper jaw, he is considered unlucky to his maternal uncle. To remedy this, the mother goes out of town, from the other side the maternal uncle comes and the ceremony 'The charm of the teeth' is performed with charity of wheat flour, white cloth and four iron nails. A time is fixed and a place appointed for the ceremony. The child's mother goes to the place, outside the village, on the road that goes to her brother's house. When the brother hears about the arrival of his sister, he brings with him an old copper coin with an iron nail, but nothing else. When the brother is approaching, the sister takes her child up in her arms, so that his face is toward the way on which her brother is coming. The brother comes silently and opens the mouth of the child, touches its teeth with the coin and the iron nail, without showing himself or seeing his sister's face. He then buries the coin and the nail on the spot and returns home. The ill luck for the maternal uncle is thus said to have been remedied.

Confinement and post birth rites

To prevent mischief to the mother or the child, a number of precautions are taken during the confinement:

(a) The confinement room should be a secluded place, so that the pain of labour should not make any noise, lest publicity increases their severity. On no account should a cat be allowed in the room nor should the mother hear one call.

(b) The universal custom in rural areas is to effect the delivery on the ground, where fire is kept and a lamp must be kept burning all night. If the lamp blows out, it is an ill luck for the child.

(c) Grains, as an emblem of good luck and water, as a purifier, are kept near the bed.

(d) A weapon, as a protector against evil, should be kept close by the mother.

(e) The house should not be swept with the broom, lest the luck be swept away. No drain should be kept open, lest ill luck enters by an aperture, which must be dirty.

The umbilical cord is cut with a sharp knife, in villages by a sweeper and in cities by a midwife. The *secundines* are buried in a corner of the house.

If a mother dies within thirteen days of her delivery, it is believed that she will return in the guise of a malignant spirit to torment her husband and family. To avert this, *Shanti Yagnye* is performed at her funeral. Just after her death, 4 nails are driven into the ground round the corpse, and when it is taken from the house door to the burning ground, rape seeds are scattered all the way behind it.

Sutak or *Chhut* or the period of impurity varies from 10-30 days; ten days among Brāhmins and twelve among Kshatriyas, 15 among Vaishyas and thirty among Sudras, thus varying invariably with the purity of the caste. But in practice the period of impurity is at the maximum of thirteen days. Neither mother nor the child should come out of the confinement room for thirteen days.

On the thirteenth day, the mother gives her old clothes to the midwife/sweepers, sometimes shared by the barber's wife. The barber's wife (*nain*) brings cow's urine, sprinkles it with grass around the mother, burns an incense and pares her nails for the first time since her confinement. Then the mother puts on her slippers and walks out of the room with the child in her arms. She is received outside the room by a menial with a pot of water and some green grass. In the outer room, an idol made of cow dung is made, covered with a red cloth and the mother worships it as a Goddess. Only women are present on the occasion and no man or Brahmins are allowed. The girls are fed and there is a lot of drum beating.

In between, there are a number of rites performed on other days:

Third day: On this day, the mother comes out of her confinement room at an auspicious hour fixed by a Brāhmin. Grain is offered by the women, which is touched by the mother of the child. Songs are sung. Jaggery is given to all women. Menials get their dues. The barber puts blades of *dubh* grass (cynadon dactylon) in the turban of the child's forbears, in order they may multiply like grass. The mother bathes on the third, fifth or the seventh day. And Churi (baked flour, sugar and ghee) is distributed among the females of the brotherhood.

Fourth day: In some regions, the mother is bathed on the fourth, seventh, thirteenth, twenty-first, thirtieth and forty-eighth day.

Fifth day: Excluding the bathing, if already taken, the ceremony on this day consists of a bath and making of a foster brother out of cow dung and grain, sweets and bread paced beneath it. It is covered with a red cloth, which is given to the midwife. The mother is given a bath with milk and cow's urine. The barber's wife plaits her hair. The yard is mopped with cow dung. The mother then enters her room that has been cleaned and plastered with cow dung. The rice, loaves and sweets are distributed among the brotherhood. The grain and money brought by visiting women is distributed between the midwife and the barber's wife.

Sixth day: The ceremony called the *Chhati*. It is a day of worship of *Shashti Devi*. Her role, importance and worship have been described in details in *Brahmvayvartey Purāna*. Lord Viśnu said, "The sixth part of nature was established as Shashti." She was the benefactor of children and was the mysterious illusion of Lord Viśnu, imparting benefits to the children. This Goddess imparts long life, protection and safety to the children. By virtue of her mythological yogic powers, she is always near the infants. On the sixth day, the mother bathes and purifies herself and observes a fast throughout the day. At sunset, she is given some rice, etc. to eat. A vigil through the night is maintained. A paper and writing material are kept ready. It is believed that the Goddess will come, sometime in the night, and write the fortune of the infant.

Seventh and tenth days: In some areas, these days are celebrated when the mother takes a bath, worships a lamp placed before the idol placed on a pile of grain. She is clad in new clothes on this occasion. Each woman of the neighbourhood gives her a coconut and five dates on the tenth day. Lastly the idol is taken away and placed under a palm tree. The kinsmen are feasted.

Thirteenth day: is very important, as already described. The mother is bathed. All earthen vessels in the house are broken or replaced. Clothes are washed, the house is plastered, Brahmins are fed. Occasionally the child is named this day.

A month after: A month or so after the birth of the child, a rite called *Daghar* Puja (Well worship) is observed. If the mother is very weak, unable to walk a distance to the well, other women of the house put a jar by her, and they carry it to the nearest well, singing songs as they go. The well is worshipped, rice and *dubh* grass are offered. On their return, menials get rewards. If the mother is fit to go, a pot of water is placed on her head and the party walks to the nearest well and it is worshipped. In some cases it is observed in the house itself.

Suckling: Immediately after birth, the midwife washes the child in a vessel, on which her reward is placed. The midwife then gives it to the mother. The child is not allowed to suckle for one and a half days. However, right after birth, a little honey is placed in the mouth of the child. Suckling the child for the first time is an occasion for a curious rite. At sunset, the midwife washes the mother's breasts with water, using some grass leaves as a brush. Some jaggery is applied to the lips of the child and suckling allowed. Some other females also wash the breasts and all of them get money as reward. Fosterage is not very common.

Clothing the child (*Chola*): The time of putting on clothes on the child varies from the first day to the thirtieth day. No special ceremony is usually held on this occasion, but the midwife and the barber's wife get rewards. On this day, in some regions, family God's temple or some Muslim shrine is visited.

Chhuchhak: On the birth of the child, the parents of the mother send sweets, clothes, ornaments for the mother, the child, and her husband.

Hijra (Eunuch): Although there is no religious observance in this, but this aspect of the visit of the *Hijras* on the birth of a child is of universal application, in all communities of India. How they know of a birth of a child and what system they adopt for the purpose is still a mystery. During British regime, some administrators thought of eliciting their help in the maintenance of birth registers. However, when a child is born in any family, a group of Hijras, clad in gorgeous saris, visit the house where the child has been born. They sing, dance, hold the child in their hands, bless the child and demand rewards, which varies according to the status of the family and sex of the child. The demand is greater when a male child is born. They give their blessings for a long life of the child and for the prosperity of the family. Their visits fall on all auspicious occasions in the family, on childbirth, marriages, and even on entry into a new house. They are not awaited but all the same they are welcomed. If a eunuch is born, Hijras take it away.

Festivals: *Lohri* in January and *Diwali* in Oct-Nov, are celebrated with special pomp and show after the birth of a child. Greater illumination than usual is done on such first occasion of the child. The next *Sanskara* (Sacrament) name giving (*Nam Karan*) is regarded as a solemn religious ceremony of importance.

CHAPTER VII

Name Giving Ceremony

OF ALL the *Sanskaras* (Sacraments), the first four, viz., *Garbhadana, Pumsavana, Simantannayana* and *Jata Karman* (Birth ceremony), which are only partially performed with proper rituals in the present days, the fifth, *Nam Karna* or name giving ceremony, is still observed with great sanctity.

This ceremony takes place on the tenth or eleventh day after the birth of the child. The present custom of name giving ceremony, in some places of India, is performed on the day when the child is first fed with a little rice (a custom in Bengal).

In order to secure good fortune, it was thought essential that a boy should be named after some God, e.g., Krishna, Gopala, Rama, Rama Chandra, Narayana, Shiva, Shankara, Ganesa, or the name may indicate God's servant (devotee) as Rama Dasa, Krishna Dasa, Lakshmi Dasa.

In some names, a combination of two Gods was given as Shiv Narayana (Shiva and Visnu). In some names, the honorofic affix *ji* was affixed as Rama Ji, Shiva Ji, under the belief that ji means to conquer or *Jiv* means to live. Moon (Chandra) is believed to bring good luck and so is affixed to many names as Moti Chandra, Gopal Chandra, etc.

Some Hindus are named after the names of springs and trees as Ganga Ram, Nemi Chand, etc.

This fact is utilized by the magicians (*Tantriks*). A favourite spell is to boil some water from a spring having the same name as the victim, thereby causing him to get into 'hot water' in the figurative sense. Another way of injuring an enemy is for the magician to drive a nail into a tree, which bears his name and thus causes him to incur some physical injury.

If a man's children do not live, he gives the newborn opprobrious names such as Khota Ran (Khota=donkey), Giddar mal (Giddar=jackal), Chuha (rat), Lota Ram (Lota=earthen vessel). Similarly, the girls are named as Billo (cat), etc.

In the present day, as in ancient times, the names of the girls like those of boys are often taken from those of Goddesses such as Lakshmi, Durga, Sita, Radha, or from sacred rivers as Ganga, Yamuna, Krishna; or from celebrated women like Savitri, Yasoda, Subhadra, etc.

Names after jewels and precious stones are also given as Mani Ram (Mani=pearl), Moti Sagar (Moti=mukta) or after the names of flowers as Padma (Padma=lily), Gulab Rai (Gulab=rose). Names of some girls are affixed after aesthetic views such as Sundari (beautiful).

In selecting the name, it is always kept in view that the names of the evil doers should not be given, such as Duryodhan, Ravana, Shakuni, etc. A Hindu always tries to maintain a calm and peaceful atmosphere in the house. He does not like that the name of evil should sound in the house and thus make the environment impure.

In order to avert an evil eye, a fair child is to be called black (Krishna). A parent will sometimes give an ugly or inauspicious name to avoid the evil eye. They name their baby in such a way owing to a superstitious belief that the child's beauty may excite the envious glances or evil eye of malicious persons. This may put the child or the family in lot of troubles. For it is remarkable that when a family has suffered early bereavement by death, it is attributed to evil influences exerted through the instrumentality of human eyes.

Types of names

There are three types of names given to a Hindu child. One is a family name, commonly known and addressed in conversation, e.g., Kaka, Kakeye, Munna, Launda for boys and Munna, Laundya, Kaki, etc. for girls.

The second name is the one which the infant receives as a private name considered as its real name, which is whispered inaudibly by the parents or the family Guru (Priest) and not revealed to others. The idea is that a man's name is in some mysterious manner connected with his personality, and the object of concealing it is to protect him from the power of the sorcerers, who are unable to injure him unless they know and can pronounce his real name. A similar superstition prevails among the Blacks, Abyssinians and Australians.

In addition to the common and the secret names, there is a third one—an astrological name. Hindus have great faith in astrology which investigates the action and reaction existing between the heavenly bodies and the rest of manifested nature and the effect of the *Nakshatras* (constellations). It enables man to know himself, to grapple with his nature. It makes him alert to utilize his abilities to the maximum. Astrological horoscope affords a man a clue to the direction he is likely tc take in various affairs of life.

The Hindus believe in the effect of the stars—Nakshatras, prevailing at the time of the birth of the child. Therefore, a horoscope (*Janam Patra*) is entrusted to be prepared by an astrologer (*Jyotishi*). The horoscope is to be drawn up in accordance with the exact time of the birth of the child, its nativity, the constellation under which it was born, with a prophecy of the duration of its life, and the circumstances, good or bad, of its probable career. It is always written by hand in Sanskrit, usually on paper with black ink, on a long roll, which may even run to sixty yards. It sometimes takes months to prepare and the Jyotishi extracts good amount of money, depending upon the richness of the parents.

The name given in the horoscope is the *Nakshatra* name, and not the one given at the name giving ceremony.

A genuine horoscope is hereby reproduced from Monier William's book, *Religious life in Ancient India,* to give the reader an idea about a horoscope:

"Adoration to the Sun. May the sun and all other planets, stars and constellations prolong the life of him for whom the horoscope is prepared.

Let the series of characters which is written by the Disposer of all things on the forehead of the child, and which is another name for astrology, be seen clearly by eyes, purified by the same science.

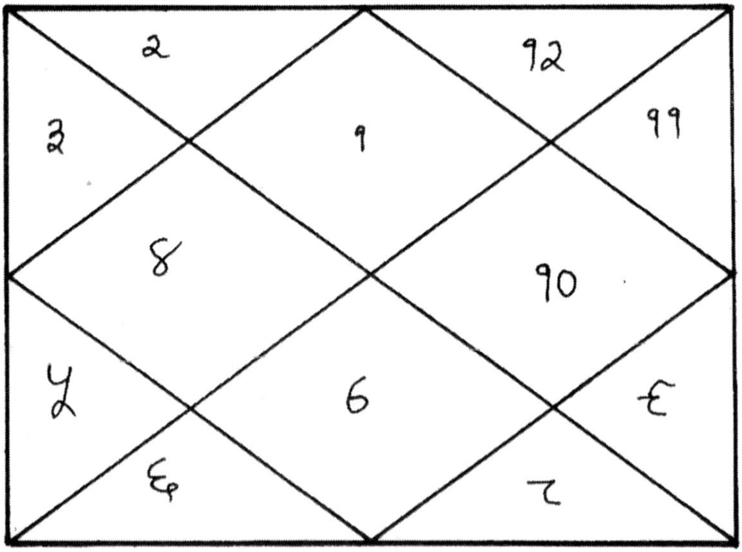

Janam Patra

May good fortune smile on the instant which came to pass after 1784 years 7 months 26 days, 22 *dandas* and 27 *palas* of the era styled the *Sakabda* had passed away, or after 1269 years, 7 months, 28 days, 22 dandas and 27 palas of the era styled the *Sana* had passed away."

"First, the measure of the day of the birth is 26 dandas, 35 palas, 0 *vipala*, and of the night is 33 dandas, 25 palas, 0 vipala; of half the day, 13 dandas, 17 palas, 30 *vipalas* and of half the night 16 dandas, 42 palas, 30 vipalas; of a fourth part of the day, 6 dandas, 38 palas, 45 vipalas and of fourth part of the night 8 dandas, 12 palas, 15 vipalas; of an eighth part of the day 3 dandas, 10 palas, 22 vipalas; and of an eighth part of the night 4 dandas, 10 palas and 37 vipalas."

"The moment of his birth being next after the 27th *pala*, after the 22nd *danda* of the day, the child was born in that eighth part of the day, which was presided over by the planet *Sukra* (Venus) and in that danda of the day, which was presided over by *Rāhu*, and consequently the aspect of Rāhu was then not such that it could have had its position in the same degree with the constellation of the child's birth or with any of the coordinate constellations.

At the instant following the 27th pala, after 22 ḍandas of the 27th day of the solar month of *Agrahana* (Nov-Dec), being a Thursday and the 5th day of the fortnight succeeding the full moon, in that *lagna* or period, during which the constellation Aries was visible in the sky, and which was ruled over by the Mars, in that half of the lagna, which was guarded by the moon, and in that third part of the lagna, which was governed by the Jupiter .... the second son of .... was born under the star *Aslesha* and when the moon had revolved to the constellation Cancer."

"The child, who will live a long life and be capable of attaining to great prosperity, belongs to the *Devari gana* or demon class, and to the *Vipra varna* or Brahmin caste and his astrological name is Harihara Devasarma. To him doth this horoscope of happy results belong."

"As the deity presiding over his birth lagna is propitious, the child will turn out to be a person of good disposition and a favourite of fortune, he shall beget many sons, and have ample dwelling places, enjoy pleasures, and possess gems of various descriptions."

"Now are to be described the planetary periods according to the birth star of the child. He was born under the star Aslesha and hence 2 years 4 months and 12 days of the same remained, at the date of child's birth. The result of this shall be the gain of clothes by the boy.

The age of the boy will be 1 year 4 months 12 days at the expiration of the period of the Moon; 9 years 4 months 12 days at the expiration of the period of Mars, which is 8 years; 26 years 4 months 12 days at the expiry of the period of Mercury, which is 17 years; 36 years 4 months 12 days at the expiration of the period of Saturn, which is 10 years; 55 years 4 months 12 days at the expiration of the period of Jupiter, which is 19 years; 67 years 4 months 12 days at the expiration of the period of earth's shadow, which is 12 years; 88 years 4 months 12 days at the expiration of the period of Venus, which is 21 years. (The total age comes to 87 years)."

The horoscope is a very important document in the life of a Hindu. It is admissible as a legal document as the proof of age. It is consulted and compared with that of the bride at the time of the selection for marriage before betrothal. It is referred to from time to time when any untoward happening occurs. It is a life time guide for the individual for his fortune.

In the present times, due importance is not given to this document by the present generation, who either do not get it prepared or do not be much guided by it. However, horoscope, being a forecast of a person's future from diagram (drawn by the astrologer) showing the relative position of the stars at birth, is a very reliable document, depended upon by orthodox Hindus.

Nam *Karan Sanskar*, performed on the 10th-11th day, of the birth of the child or other days, as described earlier, is a simple ceremony where the priest names the child, in the presence of the family members. The Brahmin is given food on this occasion, which is attended by near relatives.

According to Manu, Nām Karan of each caste should be made in a different way. The name signifies luck, power, education and behaviour.

In old days, the child was named in accordance with his name, caste, God, tribe village, devils and demons, but is no longer in practice.

However, the names in Southern India still show the name of the father, and the village in some names before the name of the individual, the caste being suffixed.

No hard and fast system prevails in naming. The caste/sub-caste suffixed is very misleading in the names of the present times.

Annaprasana (food giving), *Chooda* Karan (Tonsure), *Karn Bheda*, *Upanayana* are some other sanskaras, before the important *Sanskara* of marriage. These have been described in chapter I of this book. These are not so important in the present times in the life of a Hindu.

CHAPTER VIII
Building Ceremonies

IN SOME villages, *Bhumiya* Spirit, 'Earth Spirit' is commonly propitiated. It is supposed to be the spirit of the founder of the village. If the village or a site has been devastated — deserted by its inhabitants, people will not dare to settle there any new colony or a house without going through a careful process of propitiating the earth spirit, who never, under any circumstances, quits his old haunts. Even if no desertion is rumoured, *Bhoomi Puja* (Earth worship) is done before laying the first brick on the foundation. The ceremony is simple, performed in the presence of the Brahmin. Sweets and a piece of silver/gold metal are first put in the foundation, already dug, and then bricks are placed over it. As the south of India is the only region in which *Śaivism* is particularly prevalent, so also it is among the inhabitants of the south that devil worship is most systematically practised. No one who has travelled in that region can doubt that demonophobia is a disease with which the whole southern population is almost hopelessly and incurably afflicted. The possible reasons could be that when the Dravidians invaded India, they found the south inhabited by aboriginal savages, whose whole aspect and demeanour appeared to them to resemble those of devils. When the Aryans advanced towards south, they found it occupied by aboriginal tribes and their excited imagination concerted these powerful enemies into supernatural giants, and the most formidable of them into veritable demons (*Rakshasas*). In due course, the Dravidians, Aryans and the aborigines got blended together, but the dread of demon foes remained and this dread still prevails not only in the south, but also in other parts of India. The fear of the devil spirits of the south is so deep rooted in the minds of the people that the doors of the houses are never allowed to face the south, lest the entrance of some dreaded demon should be facilitated.

A southern aspect of the building is unlucky. Such a house will generally remain empty. Such a house has a lower selling value than the one with any other aspect. Builders make every effort to avoid a southern aspect. From astrological point of view, if the builder is Aquarius, Libra or Scorpio, his house must face west; if Taurus, Virgo or Capricorn, his house can face south; if Pisces, Gemini or Cancer, his house should face north. The house must never face east. North and south are also unlucky, as north brings poverty and the south admits demons. So, if a house must face north, east or south, then it is made to face north east, north west, south east or south west. A house built in front of a tree or facing a tank or river, except Ganges, is considered unlucky.

Times for building

Phalgun (Feb-Mar) and *Baisakh* (Apr-May) are the lucky months for building a house. *Sawan* (Jul-Aug) provides sons, *Kartik* (Oct-Nov) brings gold and silver, and *Poush* (Dec-Jan) finds worship acceptable to gods. The unlucky months are *Ashadd* (Jun-Jul), *Bhadon* (Aug-Sep), *Asauj* (Sep-Oct), *Maghar* (Nov-Dec), *Magh* (Jan-Feb), *Chetra* (Mar-Apr) and *Jeysth* (May-Jun). Ashadd breeds mice, Bhadon makes the owner ill, Asauj produces family quarrels, Maghar produces debts, Magh creates danger of fire, Chetra brings ill luck and Jeth loss of money spent on the building. The sign of zodiac also needs to be considered before undertaking construction of the building. The auspicious moment is predicted by the Brahmin.

Foundation Ceremonies

As already stated, in an auspicious moment the foundation is laid with some sweets and a silver/gold piece under the first brick. In some places, a betel nut for fertility and a *Pranda* (a silk ribbon for tying women's hair) is also placed for longevity. In some places, water from the Ganges is put into a jar and placed below the first brick. In some regions, the custom is to pour oil on the spot. In a pit dug on the spot, mangoes, betel leaves with an iron peg driven through them into the earth, curd, *Barfi* (a sweetmeat), and *Gur* (jaggery) are placed. The gods and serpents are worshipped and the pit is closed with five or seven flat bricks.

The object of the various articles used in the foundation ceremony are mangoes for fertility, betel leaves for a gentle temper, the iron peg for strength of the foundation, the coconut for prosperity in food grain and money, silver or gold for affluence. The jaggery and curds are offered to the gods. Rape seeds and asafoetida are placed to ward off evil spirits. The foundation ceremony of the house is restricted to family members, but for public buildings it is a showy affair with a lot of invitees.

Door frames

When the foundation has been built up and the building comes to plinth stage, door frames are set up. In the door frame, a black thread of wool with a bag of madder (a herbaceous plant with yellow flowers, which gives a red dye from its roots) is tied to avert calamity and for the prosperity of the inhabitants. Jaggery is distributed among the masons and the labourers. .At every step of the construction of the house, the fear of calamity and bad luck is kept in mind and remedial measures are taken to avert any ill luck. The gods are worshipped. Five or seven impressions of the hand in red are then made on the frame to signify the completion of the rites. The door frames are guarded till the construction reaches the walls (top of walls), so that any evil spirited woman may not bewitch the frame and cause death or injury to the owner. In some regions, figure of five gods is carved on the lintel of the frame for the protection of the inmates.

The form of the house

It is unlucky to build a house broader in the front than at the back. Such a house is called lion mouthed — tiger mouthed. To be lucky, a house should be cow mouthed or broader behind than in the front. A house is considered lucky if there are equal number of sides four, six or twelve. A house with its front higher than its back is considered unlucky. The owner is liable to spend more than its estimate in such a house.

In the construction of the roof, the beams of the upper storey must not cross the rafter of the lower storey, but should lie parallel to it. Rafters are counted in sets of three, the first set being the lord of the dwelling, second known as Raj for Indar (the rain God) and Yama (the God of death). On no account the last rafter should be the third (Yama's), as that would bring death or adversity. Between the months of Ashadd (Jun-Jul) and Kartik (Oct-Nov), the gods are believed to be at rest and no structural alteration should be made during this period.

Completion ceremonies

As the house approaches completion, a betel nut and an iron ring (Horse shoe) are tied to a beam in the lintel of the door. The iron ring is a protection against evil spirits. A blackened, earthen vessel is hung outside in front of the house and a hand is painted on it to avert the evil eye. A staircase should be so planned as to be on the left of the house and should have an odd number of steps.

Ceremonial decorations with the figures and designs, having a meaning of its own, are drawn by women (never by men) on the walls and inside the house. These decorations are made at the time of some festivals. One very common design is of the Swastika, drawn on the outer door wall. The traders write *Shuddh Labh* (Honest profit) on the other side of the door wall. The four lines crossing each other horizontally and vertically, making the sign of (+), represent gods of the four quarters viz. Kuber (north), Yama (south), Indra (east) and Varuna (west). The four additions upwards and sideways on the (+) represent the gods of the half quarters viz. *Isan* (north east), *Agni* (south east), *Vayu* (north west) and *Nairit* (south west). In the centre sits Ganapati (Ganesa), Lord of divine hosts. Swastika is a sign to bring luck, to avert the evil eye (when drawn in black) and to avert evil spirits (drawn after Holi/festivals).

Bandarwal: It is properly a string of *Siras* or Mango tree leaves which is hung at the entrance door of the house as a sign of rejoicing. On all other auspicious occasions like *Diwali* festival, child birth or *Swagat* (welcome) ceremonies, Bandarwal is tied on the front door. In certain regions, Bandarwal of red flowers is tied all around the house on the first of Baisakh (14 April) to invoke the blessings of God on the New Year's day i.e. first of Baisakh. On a wedding also, a Bandarwal of saffron flowers is hung on the house walls.

Thāpa: It is an important impression of a hand, popularly representing the hand of the ancestors raised in blessings on those who pay them homage. In the *Shāstras*, Thāpa represents the hands of Asvi, the God of wealth and Pusha, the God of intelligence. Thāpa is made in red on the outer walls of the house during the weddings. Thāpa is a sign of rejoicing. In Haryana, five or seven Thāpas in red beside the house door denote the birth of a boy or a wedding in the family. A single Thāpa in yellow with another drawn

Decoration

in *Ghee* (clarified butter), denote that a vigil (*Jagrata*) is being kept in honour of the house Goddess. Thāpas stamped with turmeric, *Roli* (red) or Ghee denote rejoicing. At weddings, Thapas are placed on both the bride's and bridegroom's houses. In a wedding, immediately after the seven encirclements, the Thapas are worshipped by the newly married couple and at the bridegroom's house, before entry of the bride.

In Gujarat, a circle, nine inches in diameter, is made with cow dung to the right of the door of the shop. This is plastered with cow dung on every Sunday and incense is burnt in front of it to bring honourable profit in business.

Store houses and godowns, meant for storing food grains and other treasures are invariably ornamented. The decoration suggests that the aid of some protecting power is invoked. The outer edge is enclosed with a square beading of notches in three longitudinal and five transverse lines alternately, making a continuous chain. The corners are furnished with a pentagonal lozenge with a dot in the centre. An adaptation continued all round, but occasionally in the upper centre for five consecutive times. The five transverse notches are left out, and the three longitudinal ones are made into figures of three tongues, turned about alternately, by including two notches to an angle and making the third spring out of it. Beneath the beading and the four corners, a Swastika is added without the regular additions, but represented with four dots, which suggests the modern four *Vaisnava* innovations.

The door is surrounded by a double beading of a square, topped by a larger one with trefoils in the three corners and two serpents with their heads back to back in the centre. Their eyes are dots, but the symbol is incomplete without the mystic three. Hence a dot is placed between the two heads, so as to form the triangular apex. The trefoils are double, the lower being the larger of the two showing a dot on each leaflet, where the upper one has only two dots, one in the centre and one in the stalk. A godown for storage of grain, is ornamented with the Sun symbol, a circle with curved radii or spokes, showing rays of the sun.

Ceremonial decoration on festivals

Though we shall deal with the festivals later, it is of interest to point out the ceremonial decorations made in the house on the occasion of different festivals. These decorations are all made by women in the family and are not entrusted to painters and decorators. On *Solono* day, before *Raksha bandhan, Soni* is drawn on the walls of the house in red. On Nag *Panchami* (5th of lunar Baisakh) the figure of serpent is drawn in black on the wall of the house. In lunar Kartik and Diwali, the figure is drawn below the family temple in the house in red *Geru* (red ochre). It is a veneration to Radhika and Lakshmi, the Goddess of wealth. On *Dev Utthan*, the day when gods awake from sleep in the month of Kartik, the figure in sketch is drawn in the courtyard of the house and worshipped. It is in worship of Narayana (Visnu). Figures of birds and animals are drawn in white dots on the house walls. Figures of gods are also drawn.

In the house of every Hindu of whatever status he may be, a corner in the house is earmarked for worship. The place is decorated and its sanctity maintained. In the house of the rich, a small room is allotted as the temple of the family. But in most of the houses, an altar is fixed in the corner of a room, on which the image of the family God is installed. Even if an image is not installed, a picture of the deity is hung. Worship is done, after morning bath and in the evening by a lit lamp and burning of incense called *Aarti*. However busy one might be, every member bows down before the deity at any time of the day. At the time of festivals this place is specially decorated.

The deity worshipped, mostly in the north is K'rsna and in the South Venkateswara, both are the incarnations of God Visnu. Ganesa and Lakshmi are installed at the time of Diwali in north. Rama and Sita with Lakshman are other common images installed in the north. In the South Siva (Nataraja) and Kartikeye (Subrahmanayam) are commonly worshipped as family deities. Among the Maratha people, the installation is generally of five consecrated symbols representing the five principal Hindu gods: the two stones (*Salagrama*, and *Bana Linga*) symbolizing Visnu and Siva; a metallic stone representing the female principle in nature (*Sakti*); a crystal representing the Sun (*Surya*) and red stone representing Ganesa (the remover of obstacles).

In the house or in the courtyard of orthodox Hindu families, sacred *Tulsi* plant is planted on a raised platform, where women of the house offer adoration.

Occupation Ceremonies

Before occupation, a Brahmin is asked to fix the *Mahurat* or a lucky day and time for occupation/entrance into the house. Seven or eleven days, previous to the auspicious day, the Brahmin performs *Yageye* (Havan) everyday, inside the house. On the day fixed for entrance, green leaves from seven trees, mostly mango, are tied on the outer door. The gods are worshipped, Havan is performed, figures of five or seven gods are drawn on the ground; Ganesa is worshipped.

After pouring a little oil on the threshold, the master and his family enter at an auspicious moment, carrying a new jar full of water, flowers, Gur (Jaggery), yellow thread, fruit, nuts, while the housewife carries a jug of curd. The master wears new clothes and covers his head. Both man and wife, together with a quiet milch cow, are led by a girl wearing a red cloth on her head. Brahmins and kinsmen are fed on the occasion. In some regions Ganesa is painted in red on the outer wall of the house. In the north, the *Katha* of Sateye Narayan (Visnu) is recited.

Dread of Evil Eye

In Eastern regions, the dread of the Evil Eye, responsible for some squalor, exists. Therefore when a house is built, it is considered unwise to finish it, it is safer to leave a beam projecting from a wall, or part of the front left unplastered, so that the malignant passerby, may find occasion for amused contempt, rather than for unstinted praise of the owner. Building is an act of virtue, and the heir can win no merit by completing his father's design; he prefers to leave the old dwelling incomplete and build a new one elsewhere. The superstition in the same way affects native art by insisting on irregularity of pattern and an occasional error in outline. Many or indeed most of the Eastern art patterns represent devices to repel the 'Evil Eye'.

CHAPTER IX

The Pilgrimage: Holy Places

THE PILGRIMAGE is a journey by the one, who undertakes travelling to sacred places, as act of religious devotion. On pilgrimage, Mrs. Basant says, "Places may be made sacred by the old saints living in them, whose pure magnetism, radiating from them, attunes the whole atmosphere to peace giving vibrations." Sometimes holy men or beings will directly magnetize a certain place, as by incarnations of Lord Visnu. In such places, even careless worldly men will sometimes feel the blessed influence, and will be temporarily softened and inclined towards higher things (thoughts). This is the rationale of places of pilgrimage, of temporary retreats into seclusion; the man turns inwards to seek the God within him, and man is aided by the atmosphere created by thousands of others, who before him have sought the same in the same place. In such a place, there is not only the magnetization produced by a single saint, or by the visit of some great being of the invisible world; each person, who visits the spot with a heart full of reverence and devotion, and is attuned to its vibrations, reinforces those vibrations with his own life, and leaves the spot better than it was, when he came to it. No wonder, then, that every pious Hindu is ambitious of accomplishing at least one pilgrimage, which he regards as a portion of heaven let down upon the earth. And if he can happily manage to die within the magic circle of what is called *Panchakosi* (within a circuit of ten miles round the centre of the holy city), even if one is a criminal of any religion and howsoever grave his sin may be, death within that circuit, gets immediate transportation to the heaven of Śiva.

Pilgrimage is always undertaken for some special purpose. Generally the whole family, down to the youngest baby, takes to the road with every movable thing: cooking utensils, drinking water vessels and sleeping mats, wheat flour/rice, pulses, etc. so that they can provide for themselves fully, because at the places of pilgrimage there is usually a lot of rush and accommodation and catering are a problem.

Pilgrimage is undertaken, when some dire calamity threatens a devout Hindu family, such as severe illness of the only son, a pending law suit, sick cattle or lack of rain; the main reason is at the desire of old parents, who wish to undertake pilgrimage through their son and before their death. The belief in supernatural Beings, whose influence can be obtained or warded off by various ceremonies and pilgrimage, does not interfere with the belief of the Hindu in one supreme God, in whom are invested all ultimate powers.

In every village, city or a locality, there is a place where Hindus go for worship and pilgrimage. In India, there are sacred rivers, seas (lakes, glaciers), *Puris*, mountains and temples which are places of pilgrimage, but chiefs among them are mentioned here.

In Braham *Purāna*, thousands of places of pilgrimages have been mentioned such as *Naag Tirath, Matriti* Tirath, *Shesh* Tirath, *Atam* Tirath, Soma Tirath and so on with thousand other places of pilgrimage. But as the nomenclature has changed, as also the geographical strata, it is difficult for an ordinary traveller to trace them, so the most common ones and of greatest importance in these days have been described in short for the knowledge of the reader.

Four *Dhaams*

There are four Dhaams of greatest importance for pilgrimage. In the four directions of India viz.: Kedarnath Badrinath in the north, Rameswaram in the south, Jagannath Puri in the East and Dwarika in the West.

Kedārnath-Badrināth Dhaam

Kedārnath, situated in the Himalayas at a height of 10,500 ft. above sea level, is 384 kilometer away from Haridwar. Kedarnath with one of the 12 *Jyotirlingas* of Śiva, is amongst the premier pilgrimages in India. It was from here, a place now known as Gandhi *Sarovar*, according to the Mahābhārta that Yudhistra, the eldest of the Pāndava brothers, departed to the heaven. Kedarnath is at the head of Mandakini river, in a valley 2 and 1/2 km, surrounded by high snow covered mountain.

As the legend goes, a temple (now extinct) with 12 Jyotirlingas, was built by the Pāndavas, at the present site where Adi Sankarachāraya built the present Kedārnath temple in the 8th century A. D. behind which Adi *Sankarachāraya* lies in peace in a *samādhi*.

Bhairav temple, guarding Kedarnath temple, is on a hillock to the South. Vasuki Taal, Gāuri Kund, Son Prayāg, Trijuginarayan, Gupt Kāshi, Uki Math, Agasteymuni and Panch Kedar are places of worship, in addition to the main Kedārnath temple.

Badrināth, a citadel to Lord Viśnu, stands at a height of 3,155 meters. On the extreme austerities of Sagraa's great grandson king Bhagirathi (for the salvation of his ancestors), when Ganges was requested (Ganga, the princess daughter of King Himavan of the Himālayās) to descend on Earth, to help the suffering humanity, the Earth (*Prithvi*) could not withstand the force of her flow. Ganga, who serves at the feet of Lord Visnu, was happy in the *Swarga* (realm of

Ascetics

Viśnu) and did not wish to descend; but as it was the desire of the Lord, she had to come down from Lord Viśnu's feet, against her own wish; so she came down with such a great force as would wash away the whole earth. Therefore the mighty Ganga was split into 12 channels through the curls of Lord Siva viz.: Viśnu Ganga, Sarāswati, Alakananda, Pushpa Ganga, Dhauli Ganga, Pindar Ganga, Mandākini (Madhu Ganga), Bhagarithi, Mandakini, etc., each of these is as holy as the mother Ganges.

Badrinath is the place, where Viśnu Ganga, Saraswati and Alaknanda confluence. Lakshmi, the consort of Viśnu, loved *Badri* trees that grew at that place, so the name Badrināth. It was in these waters that Lord Śiva got absolution from the guilt of decapitating Brhama's fifth head, and her too. Sri K'rsna performed penance for ages.

Over here, there are two mountain cliffs called Nara and Narāyana (the future age Mahābhārata's Arjuna and K'rsna.) Sri Badrinath Ji temple, devoted to Lord Siva, dates back to the Vedic ages, where the wedding of Lord Śiva and Pārvati, was solemnized. In the 8th century.A.D. Adi Sankarachāraya came to Badri and restored the ancient deity from Nārad Kund and established in the Ganyr cave near Taptakund. Later the King of Garhwal built the present temple and established the deity here. Queen Ahaliya Bai of Indore covered the spire of the temple with gold in the thirteenth century. Taptakund is a hot water spring, nearby, which is the abode of Lord Agni. Other places of worship in Badrivishāl complex are Gupt Kashi (*Arddh-Narisvara* and Viswānāth temples); Panch Kedār (Mad Maheswaray; Tungnath; Rudra Nāth; Kalpanāth and Kedārnāth), established by Adi Shankarachāraya in 8th century A.D., as Joshi Math. Vyas Gufa and Ganes Gufa (where saint Vyas dictated the Mahābhārata to Ganesa); Bhim Pul (where Bhim and Hanuman met); Hemkund Sāhib (associated with Guru Govind Singh) are other places, where pilgrims offer prayers and oblations.

Ramesvaram

Ramesvaram, one of the four *Dhamas*, is in the South, on an island 8 miles long and four miles broad; which nearly connects India with Manaar and Sri Lanka. People say that pilgrims to Varānasi cannot have full merits of their pilgrimage without visiting Ramesvaram.

Ramesvaram Temple, one of the most venerated shrines in India and the third largest in South India, is a massive structure, having a majestic *Gopuram* and a 1220 meter long corridor, the largest in the world. Its ceiling is decorated with paintings. This vast oblong structure contains an immense collection of *Linga* shrines, open halls and tanks, surrounded by long and beautiful galleries and corridors, with two entrances; one from town side and the other from sea side.

About its origin by Lord Rāma, there are two legends. When Rāma reached Ramesvaram, in order to cross the sea and invade Sri Lanka, Rāma went to the seashore, to drink water. At that time, he heard a heavenly voice, "Without worshipping me, you are drinking water". Hearing this, Rāma erected a Śiva Linga out of the sea sand, worshipped and invoked Śiva to bless him for a victory over Rāvana, king of Sri Lanka and he also invoked the Lord of the Sea to pave a path for him through the sea. Siva blessed him with victory. Śiva also accepted Rāma's request to have an abode in Ramesvaram permanently in the form of *Jyotirlinga*. Since then Ramesvaram is a *Dhām*, a place of pilgrimage.

The other legend and generally popular is that, anxious to expiate the impurity contracted by the slaughter of Rāvana in the battle, which terminated in the demon's death, a great devotee of Śiva, Rāma sent Hanumān, to bring a Linga from Vārānasi, that he might erect a shrine over it and so propitiate God Śiva. But Hanuman (the monkey Deity) was so late in executing the commission that Sita prepared a Linga of sand with her own hands, and Rāma having then and there performed the ceremony of setting it up and consecrated it, proceeded to worship it. He then bathed in the sea from the neighbouring promontory at a spot that was afterwards called *Dhanush Kodi*, marked by the corner of his bow. Hence a visit to this spot is essential to a completely meritorious performance of the Ramesvaram pilgrimage. When Hanumān arrived with the Linga, he saw that the ceremony had already been performed, he was disappointed. The delay in the return of Hanumān with the Linga, was due to the fact that when Hanumān reached Varanasi, B'rhma was under meditation and Hanumān had to wait long. Out of dismay, Hanumān requested Rāma to install the Linga, brought by him. Rāma asked him to dismantle the Linga, erected by Sita. Try, howsoever he may, the Linga by Sita remained firm and Hanumān failed. Then Rāma advised Hanumān to erect the Linga brought by him near the Linga by Sita, so that one must first worship the Linga brought by Hanumān. Therefore the two *Lingās* stand side by side and are worshipped.

In this temple, there is also a mobile image of Śankara (Śiva), which is taken out in golden and silvery chariots at the time of the annual festival. In the temple precincts, there are twenty wells, which have sweet water, whereas in all wells, outside the temple, the water is brackish. Rāma, through his arrows, had pierced water from these wells, which are said to contain waters from all main sacred rivers of India viz.: Ganges, Yamuna, Gaya, Shaurab, Chakra and Kumud. In addition, there are other places of worship Bhavishan Tirath, Madhav Kund, Setu Madhav, Nandikeswar, and Asht Lakshmi Mandapa. In front of Ramesvaram temple, also are an Agastey Tirath step well as well as a Kali temple. Rāma *Jarokha*, where footprints of Rāma, are still worshipped established by Adi Sankarachāraya. Rāma Kunda, Dhanush *Koti* (where Rāma linked India with Sri Lanka with a bridge made of sand), Laxman Kund, Sita Kund and Codandrum Swami and Bhagirthi, etc. are places of worship.

A visit to the pilgrimage of Ramesvaram awards blessings worth thousand visits to other pilgrimages.

Puri: Jagannāth Puri

On the shore of Bay of Bengal, Jagannāth Puri, is one of the four Dhāmas or one of the most holy places of India. Hindu pilgrims come to see the 12th century world famous temple of Jagannāth believed to be an incarnation of Viśnu

Hadimba Devi Temple, Manali

or K'rsna. It is a great place for pilgrimages. The famous *Kohinoor*, which now adorns the British crown, was bequeathed on his deathbed by Maharaja Ranjit Singh, the last ruler of Punjab Sikh kingdom, to Jagannāth. The temple is an immense ecclesiastical institution with more than six thousand priests, warders and pilgrim guides. This temple, also called *Srikshetra*, was erected by mythological king of Avanti, Indradyumna of Surya dynasty, as commanded by

God in a dream. The present temple is the creation of king Ananga Bhim Dev in 1198 as atonement for his sin of slaying a Brāhmin. Later Gajapati king spent generously in embellishing it. This temple with 20-24 feet high wall is 670 x 640 ft. in extension. It has four entrances *Singhadwār* (lion gate), *Hastidwār* (Elephant gate) *Ashwadwār* (Horse gate) and Khanjadwār (gate for lesser people).

Jagannāth which signifies 'Lord of the Universe' is one of the titles of K'rsna, and the immense popularity of this shrine is due to the fact that the doctrine originally preached before K'rsna, was that all castes were equal. On the jewelled altar of the main temple, there are seven figures for Jagannāth Dev of the dark complexion with diamond sparkling on his forehead, is accompanied by his fair complexioned brother Balabhadra and yellow faced Subhadra, sitting between her two brothers. Besides them there is *Sudarshan* Chakra. A golden image of Lakshmi is on the left, on the right a silver image of Saraswati with Nilmadhab behind them. The principal image is a rudely carved long believed to be a Buddhist emblem, adopted for worship by the Brāhmins. It is said that God himself assumed a carpenter's form and came to carve the figure in 21 days behind closed doors. King Indradyumna out of impatience entered the room, the carpenter God vanished and the figure remained unfinished with hands and legs missing. The king then installed that figure in the temple. Jagannāth is dressed in 21 costumes, according to the phases of the moon. The *puja* ceremony is also characteristic in the sense that the pilgrims have to enter the names and addresses of their four generations in a register before offering oblations.

The country house of the God is about a mile from the temple, to which he is transported on forty feet high and 30 feet square chariot with sixteen wheels seven feet in diameter, every year on Jagannāth *Rath Yātra* festival,

The three deities of Jagannath Temple, Puri

described later.

On the North of the temple is Shewetaganga (mentioned in *B'rhma* Purāna) and *Jasheswar* temple; the pujā offered here is as much fruitful as can be attained by one crore Linga *pujas*.

Dwarika *Dheesh*

Situated in Saurashtra region is the fourth Dhām called Dwarika Dheesh, the domain of Lord K'rsna. It was a flourishing port in ancient times in the kingdom ruled over by K'rsna, Viśnu incarnate. The ancient Dwarika was situated near Kodinar. A little mound which rises on the sea shore between the mouths of the rivers Somat and Singavara, 3 miles from Kodinar, is surrounded by the ruins of the temple, which the popular Hindu belief declares to be the original Dwarika, where K'rsna resided and when transferred himself to Dwarika in Okha mandala. It was founded by K'rsna owing to constant invasions and harassment by Jorāsāngha. After slaying Kansa at Mathura, K'rsna founded Dwarika, which was created out of the receding sea (the land bestowed by the Lord of the sea on K'rsna's prayers: 12 *yojans* (one *yojan* = approximately 12,000 ft.). Nidhipati, an attendant of Kuber (the God of money-wealth) appeared on request of K'rsna and made everyone in Dwarika wealthy, because K'rsna did not want any one in his city to be hungry, down trodden, poor or a beggar. Then services of illusionary Sudharma from *Devloka* were requisitioned and established in the centre of the city, for the welfare of the residents of Dwarika (Dvaravati). Local administration was set up. Then Balrama, brother of K'rsna, married Revti, the daughter of Reyvat, (*Harivamsha* Purāna). This ancient Dwarika is said to have been destroyed by the ocean, just after the ascent of K'rsna to heaven. This ancient city, established about 5,000 years ago, has been traced out by the archaeologists in recent years.

Others say, in the *Satey Yuga* Prajāpati B'rhma, the creator, desired to measure his creation—the universe. In order to find the starting point, he threw a blade of grass in the air, which landed at Dwarika, the kingdom of Yadu, the son of Yayati. Hence Dwarika is also known as Kushasthali.

Dwarika, one of the *Saptapuris*, is one of the holiest shrines of the Hindus. The other six are Varanasi, Haridwar, Ujjain, Mathura, Ayodhya and Kanchipuram. Temple of Dwarika Dheesh or RanchhorJi has a 3.5 arms length high image of Sri K'rsna, holding the conch, *Sudrashan* Chakra or wheel, club and lotus in its four hands, seated on a silver throne studded with precious stones. Built by king Jagat Singh Rathore, in 11th century, in three segments (*Garbha* mandir, *Biman mandap* and *Natya* mandap), it is also known as Jagat Mandir.

Below the Dwarika Dheesh temple, flows the Gomti and on the island in the Gomti is the K'rsna temple, Rukmini temple and Bhadra Kāli. Immediately on entrance of Dwarika Dheesh, at the archway is an image of Ganesa (who fulfils wishes) and on the right is *Kusheswar* Śiva. The other deities are AmbāJi, PurushotamJi, AnniriddhJi, Durvasha Muni, Jambavati, Radhika, Lakshmi Nārayan, Gopāl, Sateybhama and Lakshmi.

For Hindu, a visit to any temple is a pilgrimage. Some sacred sites are considered more important than others, however, and a journey to them is longed for by most of the Hindus. Usually located on the top of prominent mountain or on river bank, source, confluence or by the sea-that is at places of passage, meeting or transition. These holy spots are associated through various myths with specific deities.

Hindus believe that a pilgrimage to these special sites and the performance of certain rites there, will yield benefits in this world and, perhaps, a better existence in the next. A pilgrimage is often made to enlist the aid of a God in solving a problem or to honour a vow made to him. These sites are also auspicious spots for consigning the remains of the dead to the waters and for performing ceremonies for the deceased and purifying rituals for a bride to be. The time for making a pilgrimage must be auspicious, and the fasting and self restraints, that usually precede the journey, as well as the hardships encountered along the way, help to discipline and purify the pilgrim.

During a pilgrimage, a devotee will usually worship the deity and purify himself in a sacred river or tank, sometimes after a ceremonial head shaving. He may also circumambulate the holy spot, give alms, listen to religious discourses and chant religious songs. Although not a traditionally recognized means of attaining release (salvation), pilgrimage is considered a good way to gain religious merit and specific boons within a life, lived according to class and caste duties.

Especially important centres of pilgrimage, for the followers of Śiva are the twelve most sacred Lingas known as the Lingas of Light (*Jyotir* Linga). Some are natural formations (Stalagmites, for example worshipped in caves); others are housed in constructed temples. The origin is a subject of a myth. These twelve are also called *Dwadash* Jyotirlingas and are 1. Kedārnāth. 2. Visveswar or Viswānāth. 3. Baidyanāth. 4. Sri Onkareswar or Amreswar. 5. Mahakāleswar. 6. Somnāth. 7. Nageswar. 8. Triyemveswar. 9. Bhim Sankara. 10. Dushmeswar. 11. Malikarjun. 12. Rameswaram.

Kumbh Fair

Kumbh *mela* (festival or fair) is a Hindu religious event, during which the position of the constellation is considered to be auspicious and a holy dip in the sacred Ganges, is believed to absolve all sin The festival is primarily celebrated at four places as:

1.Haridwar: Kumbh mela is celebrated here every twelfth year, on the banks of the Ganges when the Sun is in Aries and Jupiter comes into Aquarius.

2.Parayāg: In every twelfth year, at the *Sangam* (confluence of Ganges, Yamuna and Saraswati), Kumbh mela is held in Jan-Feb; when Jupiter is in Taurus and the Sun is in Capricorn. In every sixth year Arddh Kumbh is also celebrated here.

3. Ujjain: On the banks of the sacred Sipra river, Kumbh fair is held when the Jupiter is in Leo and the Sun is in Aries. This city was named Ujjaiyeni by Lord Śiva, after he defeated the demon Tripur, the old name Avantika (Avanti) was thus replaced. Among other kings and various important events in this town, one amazing fact is that Aurangzeb offered money to build a Hindu temple at this

The Mukteswar Temple, Bhubaneswar

place.

4. Nāsik: The Kumbh mela at Nāsik on the bank river Godavari (Gautami) when the Jupiter is in Leo an the Sun (*Suraya*) is also in Leo zodiac. Nāsik is the plac where Laxman (Rāma's brother) carved the nose (*Nasik* of Sharoopnakha, the sister of Rāvana of Sri Lanka, givin the town the name Nāsik replacing the old name Padmanagar (*Sateye* Yuga), Janasthan (Dwapar Yuga Sundar Narayana (Viśnu), Kapleswar Mahādeva (Śiva Kalar (Rāma and Laxman), temples and Parnakutir (Rāma hut) and Sitaharan Gufa (from where Rāvana stole Sita are places for pilgrimage. Kumbh mela is held every twelft year beside Godāvari at Nasik.

Kumbh Mela at every place lasts for one month, but the one at Nāsik funs throughout the year. Skanda Purāna describes the four Kumbh melas in a hymn.

Sankarachāraya Math

Adi Sankarachāraya established four *Maths* in four directions of India, where four Śiva temples were built by him, where Sankarachārayas conduct religious sermons at the present times. These acharayās conduct religious sermons at the present times. These are: (1) *Jyoti* Math in Garhwal (Uttar Pradesh). (2) Govardhan Math in Jagan Nāth Puri (Orissa). (3) Shringeri Math in Karnataka. (4) Shārda Math in Dwarika (Gujarat).

Five Sarovars (Sacred pools/tanks)

There are numerous sacred pools and tanks in India, where Hindus bathe for purity, but the following five have been mentioned in the *Purānas* as important:
(1)Bindu Sarovar at Bhubaneswar in Orissa. (2) Narāyan Sarovar in Run of Kutchh in Gujarat. (3) Mansarovar in the Himalayas. (4) Pushkar Sarovar near Ajmer in Rajasthan. (5) Pampa Sarovar in the south of Tangbhadra in Karnataka.

Sapt Puris

There are seven Puris, the importance of which from religious point of view, exists in the mind of every Hindu and a pilgrimage to which is considered fortunate by the Hindus: Ayodhya (Rāma, Laxman birth place), Mathura (K'rsna's childhood), Haridwar (Har Ki Pauri of the Ganges); Kāshi (Varanasi); Kānchi or Kanchipuram, (most ancient and celebrated Golden city, worshipped by Śaivites and Viśnuites); Dwarika and Ujjain (Avantika).

Sacred Rivers

There are seven sacred rivers in India, where every

Hindu desires to have a dip in life, even the very remembrance and desire to have a bath in these sacred rivers, is considered beneficial and removal of sins; These are Ganga (Ganges), Yamuna, Saraswati, Godāvari, Narmada, Cāuvery and Sindhu.

In addition to these, Sariyu and Payasivini (Mandakini) in Northern India and Krishna river in the South, are also recognized as sacred for pilgrimage.

Mountains

Mountains are the places, where gods appeared in one form or the other and where greatest saints, Achārayas and Rishis performed austerities. Seven are of importance as: Himalayas in the North (most of the pilgrimage places are contained in this); *Vindhyachal* (where Dasratha of Ayodhya joined in *Sambra* war, as an ally of Divodasa); Mohindra Giri (Orissa: Malayanil (*Malayr Parvat*) in Karnataka; *Sahadari* Parvat range in Mahārāshtra; Revtak Parvat in Gujarat and Aravali range in Rajasthan, where Haldighat battle took place.

Sacred Confluence of Rivers (Parayāgs)

Wherever sacred rivers meet, such confluence places are considered sacred for a bath by the Hindus and have an importance as places for pilgrimage. These are: (1) Tirath Rāj Parayāg, where Ganga, Yamuna and Saraswati meet. (2) Dev Parayāg, where Alaknanda and Bhagirathi meet. This is the main Parayag among the Five in the Himalayas. (3) Rudra Prayāg, Alaknanda and Mandākini confluence. (4) Karan Parayāg, Where Alaknanda and Pindar Ganga meet. (5) Nand Parayāg: Alaknanda and Nanda meet. (6) Viśnu Parayāg where Viśnu Ganga and Alaknanda meet. (7) Suraye Parayag: Alsarrangini and Mandākini meet here. (8) Indra Parayāg: Here Bhagirathi and Vyās Ganga meet. (9) Soma Parayāg: Soma river and Mandākini confluence here. (10) Bhaskar Parayāg: This is on Kedarnāth road, 3 km away from Bhatwadi. (11) Hari Parayāg: Bhagirathi and Hari Ganga meet here. (12) Gupt Parayag: Neel Ganga and Bhagirathi meet here. (13) Shyam Parayag: Shyam Ganga and Bhagirathi confluence at this. (14) Keshav Parayāg: Where Alaknanda and Saraswati confluence.

Except Tirathraj Parayāg, all other Parayāgs are in the Uttarakhand of the Himalayas, on the road to Kedarnāth, Badri Nāth, Gangotri and the Yamnotri.

CHAPTER X

Tribal Customs and Ceremonies

INDIA IS a country of different multiracial stocks, castes and creeds. People of many religions have made this land as their abode. The tribal groups, termed as 'scheduled tribes' in the Constitution of India, have their distinct cultural traits and levels of development. Some of them are still primitive and far from modernization. They are called aboriginals. Hindu mythology describes that Aryans invaded India and came in contact with the aboriginal inhabitants, residing in India since ages. According to L.M. Srikant (Social Welfare in India) "There are a plenty of indications in the mythological stories of Ramayana and the Mahabharata and even in the pre-Christian era that the indigenous people had to resist the impact of foreign culture. But in the course of time, all these races mixed into each other, as one composite whole. The modern form of Hinduism comprises many elements of such cultural admixture. Apart from this there are groups of people representing the primitive stage of life. They are called aboriginals."

D.N. Mazumdar defines a tribe as, "A tribe is a collection of families or groups of families bearing a common name, members of which occupy the same territory, speak the same language and observe certain taboos regarding marriage, profession or occupation and have developed a well assessed system of reciprocity and mutuality of obligations".

All tribes claim their origin from a particular object

by establishing mystic relation with it. Some claim their origin from the Moon and called *Chandravansi,* some from the Sun and are called *Suryevansi*. Similarly some tribes claim their origin from birds, animals or plants and observe their special respects towards these objects. The entire clan is designated on the name of that totemic object, which they feel that there is a peculiar bond of emotional identity between themselves and that object. Totemism, respect for the totem-object of origin, is an integrated form of all the religious, ritualistic, social and artistic features of a tribe.

Classification of Tribes

The aboriginal 'scheduled tribes' can be classified into various categories on the ground of language, area of inhabitation (geographical), physical features and according to cultural contact. According to cultural contact, there can be three groups as:

First Group, which may include those tribes who are living in the most primitive stage; such as the hill *Marias* of Bastar, the *Juangs* Keonijihar, the *Gadabas* and *Bondos* of Orissa. These hilly tribes are entirely isolated from the people of Plains. Their major characteristics are: (a) All members live a communal life. (b) All members share a similar economic structure. (c) All are concentrated round a peculiar form of agriculture. (d) They are honest, simple, innocent and are very shy before strangers.

Second Groups includes those tribes, who on one side are associated with the old traditions, but on the other they have begun to change. Such major tribes are the Marias, *Bhumias, Binijhware* and *Baigas*. Their characteristics are: (a) Individualistic village life. (b) Non participation in common affairs. (c) Adoption of the outer mode of life and the absence of primitive simplicity.

Third Group are such tribes who represent the ancient aristocracy of this country such as *Bhils, Nagas, Gond*

Rajas, *Bhuiya* landlords, *Korku* nobles and the wealthy *Santhals*. These tribes retain their old tribal name and practise their tribal religion. Apart from this, they have also adopted the faiths of modern Hinduism and modern modes of living.

Marriage and Selection of Mates

Marriage, in brief, may be classified as follows: (a) Monogamy viz. one male and one female, is the most common. (b) Polygamy viz. one male and more than one female, found among Nagas, Gonds and the Baigas. (c) Polyandry viz. more than one male to one female, practised among the Todas and Tiyans of Southern India, the Khasis of the Sub-Himalayan region.

Selection of Mates is an important affair in every tribal community. Commonly practised forms for selection are: (a) Marriage by service; this system prevailing among the *Purums* of Manipur, in which the groom serves to his bride's house for a period of three years, performing all works expected of a son in the family, with boarding and lodging free at the father in law's house. After the probationary period, he marries the bride. (b) Marriage by capture, practised by various tribes in Chhota-Nagpur among Hos, Santhals, Mundas and Bhumias and also a common method in all tribal communities. Utilization of the physical force by the bridegroom is the method, where the bride first resists, but ultimately agrees to go with the groom. In certain cases, where the bride does not agree the groom puts vermilion upon the forehead of the bride and the marriage is performed. (c) Marriage by purchase; a system which prevails among Nagas, Hos and Khasias, where the payment of the bride price is made. (d) Marriage by elopement viz. when a boy and a girl fall in love, but their parents refuse, both of them escape from the village but return after sometime and are recognized husband and wife. (e) Marriage by intrusion, practised by Santhals, Oraons and Hos. When a boy has intimate relation with a girl, but postpones marriage, the girl enters the hut of the boy stealthily and stands firm against the opposing mother in law, the marriage is performed. (f) Marriage by exchange, where the son of one man marries the daughter of the other and the son of the second man marries the daughter of the first. (g) Marriage by settlement is the most common method and prevails among the Bhils and some other tribes.

A Typical Khasi Marriage

The most remarkable feature of the Khasi marriage is that it was customary in the earlier days for the husband to live with his wife in his mother in law's house till the time his wife gave birth to one or two children. After that he could take his wife home. All the earnings of the husband became the property of the mother in law, during the period the husband lived in her house. There is no polygamy among Khasis. Ceremonially, the boy selects his life partner and after some association between the boy and the girl, they disclose to their parents. Their parents find that if there is no taboo and both the parties agree, the marriage is arranged. The age of the boy between 18 to 25 and that of the girl between 13 to 18. Exchanging the rings between the would be husband and the would be wife is common. On the fixed day, the marriage party along with kith and kins, in their best dresses and garments and wearing turbans starts from the groom's house, after feasting to the bride's house. The female relations do not accompany the bridegroom. Some male members of the bride's part, receive the marriage party on the way, welcome them and exchange 'Pan' (betel). In the meantime the bride is dressed in her best dress and jewellery. The females do not cover their heads during the marriage day. A *Ksiang* and an elderly person lead the bridegroom to the bride's house. Similarly a Ksiang represents the bride's party. A dialogue between the two *Ksiangs* is the start of the ceremony. If during the dialogue nothing transpires, that would go against uniting the two, then religious rite is performed and rings are exchanged with the declaration of the two as husband and wife. The Ksiang first enters the bride's house, followed by the groom and then bridegroom's party. The groom's Ksiang hands over the groom to the maternal uncle or the bride's father. Maternal uncle or father takes the groom and makes him sit by the side of the bride. When the formalities are completed, the person, who performs the ceremony, offers prayers to God Lei Synshar for his blessings for the couple and prosperity throughout life. Then he pours liquor three times on the ground from the gourd. Then he remembers and takes the names of all family clan members, and pours the liquor on the ground. Then he announces, before all the elders and all other people present that they all bear witness to the union of these two people as husband and wife. After entertainment, the friends and male relatives of the groom go back to their respective houses and the groom remains in the house of the bride. After 3-4 days, the bride, the husband and the female members of the family, go to the house of the husband and the bride seeks the blessings of her mother in law. After formal introduction and blessings by the elders, the husband and the wife are free to visit each other's house. Normally the wife does not stay in husband's house till she has given birth to 1-2 children. When the husband is working out of town, the wife usually stays with him. Nowadays, marriages among the Khasis are mostly on modern basis and many of the customs, ceremonies and the expenditure are cut down.

Divorce among the Khasis is not common. The main causes for divorce are adultery, barrenness and non-adjustment and noncooperation in the family. A woman will never be divorced during pregnancy. Both the parties should be agreeable for a divorce. The mother is the supreme in all household matters, which ensures security to every existence.

Marriage is an important institution in every society. It is regulated by the observance of certain rules of endogamy, exogamy, hypergamy, preferential mating and prohibited degrees. Thus a member of Santhal community may marry within his tribe, but cannot marry within his clan. The *Purumkukis* of Manipur prefer the cross cousin marriage. Similarly in some tribes, the younger brother can keep the widow of his elder brother. Thus there are various methods of acquiring mates in Indian tribes, but most of the marriages consist of one husband-one wife.

Disposal of the Dead

In Khasis, there is a humble way of describing some one's death. The death is announced by a family member after he had called the name of the deceased in his ear three times. If there is no response, the death is confirmed. When the death is confirmed, the dead body is bathed with warm water from three earthen pots, then dressed in white cloth and a turban tied anti-clock wise, as against normally clockwise. On the day of funeral, the male children of the relatives of in laws, offer a pig or money, as a token of love and respect. This is known as *Pynkham* . A rice bear is poured on the funeral pyre. Food and betel nut are also kept along the dead body, under the belief that the deceased will share the nuts with his ancestors in the heaven. Eggs are also broken on the funeral pyre. The funeral pyre is lit first by the eldest son of the deceased in the case of women only, by the eldest cousin in case of men and then by others. Three arrows in three directions (north, south and east) are shot. Relatives offer betel nuts on the pyre and bid farewell before returning home. When the body is burnt, fire is extinguished by pouring water, bones are collected in three trips, kept wrapped in a white cloth by the female relatives and are kept in earthen pot. After three days, the relatives and friends see the foot/finger prints of the departed, by which they know the future events in the family of the deceased. The pregnant women do not accompany the funeral procession. Three days mourning in the family is observed. Khasi widow or widower is forbidden to marry within one year. The female child is a must among the Khasis, because the chain of inheritance is always passing from the females. In case of accidental death, a black hen is offered, believing that if such a death is not neutralized, further death will follow in future. In case of a death by cholera, small pox or due to some other contagious disease, the body is buried for one month, then taken out and burnt.

Respect To Ancestors

The khasis remember their dead, time and again, as a respect to their ancestors. The children and relatives perform a ceremony called *Aibam,* as a token of love and affection. To ignore the dead is worst form of ingratitude, which may bring misfortune to the family.

The Khasis are firm believers in God, equality among men and women, rich or poor, belief in hard work and sincere efforts. They live a clean and moral life, respect and love their parents, uncles, elders. They do not steal, commit murder or do anything which may bring bad name to his or other's house. They do not blame God on miseries and misfortunes, but blame themselves, and thank Him for his blessings.

Jaintias practise Black Magic, which is nothing but witchcraft. Imitative Magic, most common for killing or injuring the enemy, by making his figure out of earth taken out of a grave and then injuring it gradually under the belief that by injuring the doll, the enemy also receives injuries likewise. Mapilas of Malabar also practise this. The pegs are struck into the body of the doll, which is afterwards buried in a grave, in the name of the enemy, whom it is found to injure.

Contagious Magic means that some nail parings or hairs of the enemy are taken and destroyed, under the belief that things, which have once been united, they remain in sympathetic condition, thus their destruction will also injure the enemy.

Sorcery (Positive Magic) is the art of influencing the spirits. Among all primitive tribes, it is believed that there are evil spirits, which can harm. It is believed that magic can deprive the evil spirits from their power, by which they harm others. The sorcerer does these things without the help of Gods. He makes the demon subservient to his own will. Thus one wreaks vengeance over his rivals and enemies. Such type of magic or *Tantric* cult is also being practised in Northern India. The tribes have also been influenced by Hindu *Trantic* Cult.

"The Indian approach accepts the validity of the different traditions: *Sarbangama Pramanya*. Without creating great racial disturbances, we aimed at achieving racial harmony. The authenticity of outlook marks the Indian approach from the beginning of history. We did not isolate the Tribal communities, nor did we encourage indiscriminate amalgamation" (Dr. S. Radhakrishnan). Tribals developed their own life style, own systems of philosophy and religion, belief in what life showed them and experience seemed to confirm, worship what inspired awe or admiration in them and despise what hurt their feelings, desires and ambitions. In India, every religion is honoured and tribal societies in India are free to celebrate their functions and festivals, according to their traditions, as described later.

APPENDIX

Yoga In Hindu Customs

As every science has its methods, so has every religion. The methods of attaining the end of religion are called Yoga, in Hindu customs. Different forms of yoga are adapted to the different natures and temperaments of men as Karma yoga, Bhakti Yoga, Raja Yoga or Jnana Yoga. These are all different roads leading to the same centres (Vivekananda). This practice of Yoga is as old as Hinduism. It has become a part and parcel of every Hindu custom or ceremony, since ages. Concentrating the powers of the mind is called yoga, as has been advocated in scriptures and inculcated in our customs as fasts, worship and meditation. It is claimed that by concentration of mind, every truth in the universe becomes evident to mind, both external and internal truths. That is how great saints and seers could foresee what is to come. Maya (illusion) was detected by them. Vashista or Vidur (Mahabharata) knew what is happening and what will happen.

The yoga has always been a part of spiritual science in the life of Hindus. Rishis and Munis acquired great powers by way of meditation of every variety, asceticism and yogic exercises. These powers may have been in the sphere of weaponery, foreseeing things and other divine acts which could not be done by material science. Hanuman, having learnt yoga in ashrams of rishis and munis, in childhood, used it to make his body bigger or smaller according to the need in Sri Lanka. By yogic spiritual powers, he crossed hundred yojan (vedic length) of sea, without any outside aid, but with the help of yoga about which Jamwant (the bear disguised wise minister of Sugriv in Ramayna) reminded him of his power. In the life of the Hindus, their customs and ceremonies, festivals and fairs, yoga plays a great part, as is enunciated in following paras. Yoga is based on determination by mantra (hymns) and tantra (enchantment). This power of determination (sankalp shakti) has been preached in the Vedas, wherein prayer is that one's mind should be virtuous and avoid evil.

Indian customs, manners and food habits are under the influence of yoga. White colour symbolises truth. Our ancestors used white garments for the propagation of truth. White garments are an aid in the observance of Brahmcarya and other advantage of white garments is the activation of Kundalini Shakti, by which the umblical cord is also maintained in proper position.

The Turban of the men and the head cover of the women, save them from the effects of heat and cold.

Turt of hair on the crown of the head is a perception of B'rhma cakra. The sacred thread (yagyopaveet also called B'rham Sutra symbolises the observance of the rules of Yama (Dharma). Three threads of the sacred thread represent the three attributes viz Sattva (spiritual reality) Raj (luxuriousness) and Tam (darkness) and reminding us of supreme limitless, encourage us to be virtuous. Six threads of yagyopaveet vouchsafe our control over lust, anger, greed, enchantment, intoxication and grief.

The custom of putting on a Tilak on the forehead is since primordial times. This is applied at the point of Agya Cakra, the place of the lord whioch also is the place of residence of Sada Siva. Sandalwood paste applied on the forhead is not for the self, but is for the pleasure of the Almighty, as applied on HIM.

The women recognise vermillion as an indicator of marriage and put it on wishing a long life for their husbands. The reason for this is that an Indian women recognises her husband as the only master and an above all for this adoration, she applies vermillion at the Agya Cakra. The earings of women and men have a special link with yoga, because ear is that organ through which the teaching is communicated. The blessings of Mantra are also given in the ears. The ear has an interlink with Agya Cakra, because Sushma nerve passes nearby. At the time of naming a child the name is first whispered into his ear, which he bears throughout life. At the sacred thread ceremoney, the ears are also pierced. At that time Gayatri mantra is initiated into the ears. In addition to that, ears are pulled in order to repent for anything. Because of the importance in yoga, the supreme yogi Lord Siva wore ear rings (Kundal).

Observance of fasts, which is very common among Hindus, is essential for the purification of the conscience. Purity of food is given great importance in Hindu culture because without this, path of yoga is not possible.

In all auspicious deeds, yoga has great influence. Sounding of conch, ringing of bells or beat of drums in the temples is to invoke the self evil and is an expression of B'rhma sound.

Omens, good and bad, support yoga knowledge. The worship of Sun, Moon or Agni (fire) is a kind of yoga devotion, because three nerves (Idda, Pingla, Sushamna) in yoga devotion are also called Sun, Moon and Agni respectively.

Pilgrimage to holy places is considered of great importance for salvation. Triveni at Paryag where Ganges, Yamuna and Sarswati meet is recognized very holy, so is the case in Agya cakra in yoga, where three main nerves (Idda, Pingla and Sushamma) meet. By control of Agya cakra, a person gains salvation. Pilgrimage places are such where yogis and persons, who acquired supernatural powers spent some time, gave sermons and communicated virtuous qualities, such places had been either the banks of holy rivers as Ganges, Yamuna or on the Himalyan terrain, Kailash, Mansarover, Badri Nath, Kedar Nath, Amar Nath, Pashupati Nath, Dwarka, Jagannath, Ramesvaram, Haridwar, Kashi, Paryag and Mathura.

Our various festivals and fairs represent our religious trend of mind. Every festival has some background, which gives us moral strength; Vijay Dashmi (Dussehra) implores us to be virtuous like Rama, to be self less like Bharat, and by controlling our lust, ego, anger, greed etc, one should work for the universal welfare. This festival also reminds us to overpower the evil (Ravan) and establish good will like Vibhishan. In most of the educational institutions, a morning prayer meeting is held. Students stand attention and sing natioinal song. The position of 'Attention' is to concentrate the mind. All parts of the body in this position become alert. The vertebral column and the chest are straightened, by which the mind concentrates. This is all a part of yoga. Rebirth is an established belief in Hinduisim, which is also a part of yoga. In Bhagvad Gita, K'rsna says. 'After passing many births, a yogi ridden off all sins, by efforts, gets salvation'.

Thus it is seen that Hindu culture has the influence of yoga in all minuteness.

SELECT BIBLIOGRAPHY

Aiyer VG: Chronology of Ancient India (1982)
Bahadur OL: The Book of Hindu Festivals and Ceremonies, 94
Biswick: The Hindu Gods (1993)
Blackhalm RJ: Incomparable I)ndia.
Chaturvedi LP: Ram Rajya and Its Ideals (1992)
Geeta Press: Gopal, Mohan, Sri K'rsna.
Harshananda: Hindu Gods and Goddesses (1992).
Ions V: Indian Mythology (1988).
Kalyan: Special Numbers and Monthly Magazines.
Maurice T: The History of Hindostan (1795).
The Mahabharata (Hindi).
Meena: The Temples of South India.
Naidu H: Chhatisgarhi Lok Geeton Ka Loktatvik Tatha Manovagyanik Anusheelan (1987), (Hindi).
The Puranas (Hindi).
Philadelphia Museum of Art: Ways to Siva (1982).
The Ramayana (Hindi).
Rashtra Dharam: Hindu Gaurav Vishesank.
Rose H A: The Religious Life of Indian People.
Sam Buddhananda Swami: Vedanta Through Stories (1971).
Sanga Vraman: All India Travel Companion (1995).
Savitri: Tales From Indian Classics (1990).
Singh CL & PN: Hinduism (1996).
The Vedas (Hindi).
Tourism of India: Pamphlets.
Williams: Religious Life in Ancient India (1990).
Various News Papers, Magazines and Journals.
Varshney S: Hinduon Ke Brat, Parv Avam Tyohar (Hindi 1988).

GLOSSARY

AGNI PURĀNA: Ancient holy book of Hindus. This purana derives its name from Agni, God of fire. It was originally communicated by Agni to Muni Vashista in order to preach the two fold knowledge of B'rhma.

AKSHEY: Third of Baisakh (April).

ANANT: A name of Vis'nu.

ARUNDHATI: Wife of saint Vashista.

ATRI: One of the Saptarishi.

BALARAMA: Elder brother of K'rsna.

BHAIRAVA: A manifestation of Śiva.

BHAGWAT PURĀNA: This Purāna has described ample duties of Hindus. It opens with the Gayatri. It contains events that happened to the mortals and immortals of Saraswata Kalpa.

B'RHMA: The supreme soul of the universe, self-existent, absolute and eternal, from which all things emanate and to which all return.

BRAHMIN: The first of the four castes. A Brahmin is the chief of all created beings. He is entitled to all honour, and enjoys many rights and privileges.

B'RHM PURĀNA: In the list of Puranas this stands first. Hence it is sometimes referred as Adi or First Purāna. It was recited by B'rhma to Marichi and said to contain 10,000 slokas. But the actual number is between 7,000 to 8,000.

DAITYAS: Titans. They are a race of demons and giants, who warred against the gods and interfered with sacrifices.

DURGA: Wife of Śiva; benevolent at times terrific.

DWAPAR: One of the four yugas; in this period virtue reduced to half.

GANGA: A river Goddess.

GANESA: Elephant headed God; worshipped first among all.

GARBA DHANA: Impregnation; first night after wedding; called Sohag Rat.

GOKUL: A place near Mathura, where K'rsna spent his childhood.

GREH: Household.

GURU NANAK: The first Guru of Sikh.

GAYATRI: A most sacred verse of Rig veda. It was originally a simple invocation of Sun later converted into a mystical propitiation of the spiritual origin and essence of existence. It has addressed Sun as Savitri, the generator, hence it is also called Savitar.

HANUMAN: Great devotee of Rama; warrior, emissary,

espionagist.

JAGANNATH: A name of K'rsna.

KALI YUG: The present yug commenced approximately around 3102 bc. It is the period of darkness.

K'RSNA: The name occurs in the Rig veda but without any relation to the great deity of later time. The earliest mention of K'rsna was in the Chhandogya Upanishad. The modern deity of K'rsna is the most celebrated hero of Indian mythology. He is said to be the eighth incarnation of Vis'nu.

K'RSNA PAKSH: Light half of the month when moon increases.

LAKSHMI: Wife of Vis'nu, Goddess of wealth and prosperity.

LOKA: In general the triloka or the three worlds are heaven, earth and hell. The Sankhya and Vedanta school of philosophy recognize eight lokas or regions of existance. They are B'rhma loka, the world of superior deity; Pitri loka, that of Pitris, Rishis and Prajapatis; Soma loka, that of the moon and planets; Indra loka, of the inferior deities; Gandharva loka, of heavenly spirits; Rakshasa loka, of the Rakshasas; Yaksha loka, of the Yakshas; Pisacha loka, of the imps and fiends.

MAHABHARATA: The great epic poem of the Hindus. It is probably the longest epic in the world. It is divided into eighteen parvas and contains about 220,000 lines.

MAHAVEER: Digambar Jain, 24th Tirathankar.

MATASEY: First Vedic incarnation of Vis'nu in fish form.

MOKSHA: A state of complete truth and peace. Here ends the cycle of births as one merges with the Supreme after he attains moksha.

NARASINHA: Man lion incarnation of Vis'nu.

PADMA KALPA: The last expired Kalpa of B'rhma.

PAKSH: A fortnight.

PARSHURAM: Sixth incarnation of Vis'nu; son of saint Jamdgin.

PARVATI: Wife of God Śiva; daughter of Himavan and Meyna of Himalaya.

PATALA: The infernal region inhabited by Nagas, Daityas, Danavas, Yakshas and others.

PRAHĀLAD: A devout of Vis'nu.

RAMA: Eldest son of Dasaratha, the king of Ayodhya, descendant of the solar dynasty. He is the seventh incarnation of Vis'nu.

RAVANA: A demon king of Lanka.

SARASWSATI: Wife of B'rhma, Goddess of learning and wisdom.

SATEY YUGA: First yug after the general deluge; age of transcendent purity; commenced on 3rd of Baisakh.

SAVITRI: Another name of Sun. Also name of Sateyvan's wife.

SHUKL PAKSH: Dark half of the month, when moon decreases.

SITA: Wife of Rama.

ŚIVA: The name Śiva is unknown to Vedas, but Rudra, another name of the deity, occurs in Veda and from this the great deity Śiva has been developed.

TRETA YUG: Second yug after satey yug; virtue decreased by quarter in this era, commenced on 3rd Baisakh.

TULSI: A sacred herb, worshipped by Hindus.

VAMAN: Fifth incarnation of Vis'nu, who measured all three worlds in three steps.

VEDA: The holy books, which are the foundation of Hindu Religion. They consist of the hymns written in an old form of Sanskrit and according to the most generally received opinion they were composed between 1500 and 1000 BC.

VISWAKARMA: The architect of the divinity.

YAMA: The God of death; also called Dharmaraj.

YUGA: An age of the world. It is the period of 43,20,000 years of man divided into Sat Yuga, Treta Yuga, Dwapar Yuga and Kali Yuga.